Playing for Scotland

PLAYING FOR SCOTLAND
A History of the Scottish Stage 1715—1965

DONALD CAMPBELL

MERCAT PRESS
EDINBURGH

First published in 1996 by Mercat Press
James Thin, 53 South Bridge, Edinburgh EH1 1YS

ISBN 1873644 574

The publisher acknowledges subsidy from
the Scottish Arts Council towards the
publication of this volume

Set in Garamond at Mercat Press
Printed and bound in Great Britain by
Biddles Ltd., Guildford and King's Lynn

CONTENTS

ILLUSTRATIONS

ACKNOWLEDGEMENTS

Acknowledgements are due to the following individuals and organisations whose help has been invaluable in the writing of this book: Tristram Clarke, Morag Corrie, Maggie Gordon, Ronald Mavor, Colin Morton, Helen Murdoch, Mary Pollock, Jim Pratt, Ida Schuster, Donald Smith, Tony G Vasey, Elizabeth Watson, Peter Whitebrook, Clara Young; People's Palace, Glasgow, Scottish Theatre Archive, Glasgow, Theatre Museum, London, Workers' Education Association, Edinburgh, and the staff of the Local Studies Departments at the Libraries of Aberdeen, Dundee, Glasgow, Perth and the Edinburgh Room of Edinburgh Central Library. Thanks are also due to the Keeper of Manuscripts at the National Library of Scotland for permission to quote Henry Johnston's letter to Robert Dundas and to Alan Little of the Netherbow Theatre, Edinburgh, for his assistance with the cover photograph.

BIOGRAPHICAL NOTE

Born in Caithness and raised in Edinburgh—where he still lives—Donald Campbell's involvement with theatre began in his teens, when he was employed as a stage-hand at Edinburgh's King's Theatre. Since then, his involvement has mainly been as a writer, active in Scotland over the past twenty years as poet, essayist, radio and television script-writer, occasional stage director and award-winning playwright. Best known for his plays *The Jesuit*, *The Widows of Clyth*, *Blackfriars Wynd* and *Nancy Sleekit*, he has held a number of Writer's Fellowships, including Writer-in-Residence to Lothian Schools (1975-77), Fellow in Creative Writing at the University of Dundee (1987-89) and the William Soutar Fellowship in Perth (1991-1993). In 1981, he discovered a passion for theatre history when, as Resident Playwright at Edinburgh's Royal Lyceum, he was required to write a history of that theatre for its centenary. His previous publications in this field include *A Brighter Sunshine* (1983) and *The Fraying Rope* (1992).

KEY EVENTS

1935 Perth Rep founded

1939 Dundee Rep founded

1940 First professional season at Byre Theatre, St Andrews

1941 CEMA (later the Scottish Arts Council) comes into being

1943 Glasgow Citizens' Theatre founded

1953 Gateway Company, Edinburgh, founded

1955 Self-supporting companies go out of business and the era of theatre subsidy begins

1965 Gateway Theatre loses grant and closes. Royal Lyceum Theatre Company established

Preface

PLAYING FOR SCOTLAND

The history of the Scottish Theatre, unlike that of its English counterpart, cannot be told in terms of institutions, dramatists or even plays. It is a story in which considerable difficulty, intermittent prosperity and occasional triumph are viewed within a continual, sometimes desperate, always determined, struggle. Yet, even as I write these words, it is a history that continues to unfold. Today, the vision of a truly Scottish Theatre burns as brightly as ever. That this is so is largely due to those men and women who have held the vision and who have followed it with single-minded determination.

With only rare exceptions—the poet Allan Ramsay, the playwrights Joe Corrie and James Bridie—most of these people have been actors. In seeking to tell the story of the Scottish Theatre over the last three centuries, therefore, one must inevitably give prime consideration to the central rôle played by the Scottish actor.

Acting, of course, is the most elusive of all the arts. Most artists are vitally concerned with the world in which they live, but this concern need not always be an essential element of the work. It is entirely possible—if not, perhaps, always desirable—for painters, musicians and even writers to follow a personal vision in solitude, paying little more than passing attention to the hurly-burly of the life that surrounds them. This degree of detachment is simply not available to the actor, who must use the events and mores of the day as integral parts of his or her creation. A line which would shock the audience in 1896 might deliver a laugh in 1996—and vice versa.

This makes acting the most unenviable of all the arts. Because of the essentially ephemeral nature of the work, immortality is simply not available. No matter what claims may be made for the performances of yesteryear, we can never really reach an appreciation of their true worth to the extent that we can with other artists. Even when such performances are available on film, this is likely to be as much of a hindrance as a help. Watching film of long-dead actors can often be like reading poetry in translation. We have the sight and sound of the performance but are quite unable to experience the context in which it was given—and so, to a greater or lesser extent, something is missing.

And yet, it is important that these performances—and their effect upon the audiences of their time—be recorded in some form, no matter how unsatisfactory. The art and practice of theatre involves the acceptance of certain verities which re-assert themselves continually: this is the guiding principle of theatrical tradition. Theatre is a live art in which triumph and disaster are but two sides of the same coin: if we are to create the conditions for the first, we must draw on the experience of tradition to ensure that we avoid the second.

'The purpose of playing' Shakespeare tells us 'both at the first and now, was and is...to hold the mirror up to nature.' This is as true of the actor's art in Scotland as it is in any other country. By no means all of the actors who appear in these pages were Scottish by birth—quite the contrary, in fact—but every one of them was obliged, in one way or another, to come to terms with the conditions that prevailed in Scotland at large.

Playing *in* Scotland has always involved playing *for* Scotland, not simply in the representative sense—every actor who makes his living in Scotland becomes *ipso facto* a Scottish actor—but in the competitive sense, too. Over the years, a goodly number of theatrical entrepreneurs have travelled north, seeking to win the prize of the Scottish audience while persisting in the belief that Scottish conditions are no different from those of the English provinces. The fact that such people are rarely mentioned in this narrative is not due to any innate hostility one feels towards them, but simply because such initiatives have always resulted in complete, utterly uninteresting, failure.

An awareness of the aspirations, emotions and perceptions of the Scottish community has always been a prerequisite for theatrical success. In most other countries, this principle is regarded as axiomatic; the fact that this has not been the case in Scotland tells us, in itself, a great deal about the nature of the perpetual struggle that the following chapters attempt to describe.

Donald Campbell
Edinburgh 1996

Chapter One

HONEST ALLAN'S PEOPLE

One of the most enduring attractions of an Edinburgh summer is the Floral Clock in Princes Street Gardens. Situated at the very heart of the city, it has long been a source of delight to residents and visitors alike. Literally thousands of people pause to view it every single day during the summer months, and the experience of waiting on the steps, with bated breath, for the minute hand to swing round to twelve (in order that the cuckoo may be released from its box to cheep the hour) is retained in the recollection of many generations of children.

Yet how many of these children will recall, with anything but the vaguest memory, the statue that stands *above* the clock? It is a statue of a robust little man, dressed in the informal manner of the eighteenth century, who looks out on Princes Street with a somewhat proprietorial air. Any casual visitor to the city might guess at once that this is a memorial to an Edinburgh citizen of some consequence—yet there is no explanatory plaque and even the inscription provides little information. There are no dates, no job description, only a simple representation of his name, engraved on the base of the statue in bold lettering: ALLAN RAMSAY.

Without a doubt, Allan Ramsay was, and remains, one of Edinburgh's favourite sons. Besides that statue in Princes Street, his name is celebrated by a memorial plaque at Newhall, an obelisk to his memory at Penicuik, a country hotel at Carlops and, perhaps most appropriately, a congenial public house in the High Street. Students of Scottish literature honour him, not only as a poet in his own right, but as editor of the revivalist anthologies *Evergreen* and *The Teatable Miscellany* (both 1724). Art historians know of Ramsay's contributions to visual art; his establishment of a school of painting in Edinburgh and his encouragement of his son, also named Allan, the greatest portrait painter of the eighteenth century. Architects know of Goosepie Lodge, the somewhat eccentric house Ramsay built for himself on Castlehill, where it still stands. Even librarians recognize the significance of Ramsay, who established the first circulating library in Scotland in 1728.

He was born on 15 October, 1684, in the village of Leadhills, Dumfries-shire. His father, an overseer in the local lead mine, died when he was in his infancy and his mother married again. After some education at the local parish school, he was sent by his stepfather to Edinburgh, to be apprenticed to a wig-maker. As in everything else that he did, Ramsay excelled in that trade and opened a shop in the Grassmarket sometime around 1712. Interested in litera-ture from an early age, he began writing poetry in his late twenties, his first collection appearing in 1715. By 1718 he had given up wig-making for book-selling, moving from the Grassmarket to the High Street. From then until his death in 1758, he maintained his position as one of the best-known and most influential Edinburgh citizens of his time; a man of energy and versatility, whose zealous public spirit was matched by the unflinching courage with which he carried through his schemes. His artistic integrity, together with his generous nature and a certain flair for plain speaking, earned him the nickname 'Honest Allan'.

In 1736, Ramsay opened a theatre off the High Street, in Carrubber's Close. Although it had a very short life, this theatre is important for two reasons. First, it was the first regular theatrical establishment ever erected in Scotland and so can be regarded as a significant starting-point in any history of the Scottish Thea-tre. Secondly, the company's battle for survival—and the outcome of that battle—was to have a profound influence on the conduct and affairs of the Scottish Theatre for the next two centuries.

In Ramsay's time, Edinburgh was a very different city from the one that we know today. Its population was somewhere around 40,000, most of whom were crammed into what we would now regard as the tiny area of the High Street. In crowded tenements family piled on top of family, irrespective of wealth or title, and people lived together in an essentially communal manner where private life and public life were almost indistinguishable. It was the kind of place, in short, where a theatre might be established with some hopes of success.

Ramsay's involvement with theatre began in 1719, at the invitation of Signora Violante, the celebrated Italian rope-dancer and dancing teacher, who had settled in Carrubber's Close a few years earlier. (This lady, who toured the British Isles for the next twenty years, made a major contribution to eighteenth century Theatre with her discovery of the youthful Peg Woffington in Dublin in 1727.) According to Alexander Carlyle of Inveresk, who later became one of her fa-vourite pupils, Signora Violante was impeccably respectable and would 'admit no boys of above seven or eight years of age' to her dancing lessons. However, she did need to furnish partners for her grown-up ladies and invited students from the University to take part in some of her classes, and it was with such students that she would occasionally present plays.

On the Hogmanay of 1719, a company of 'young gentlemen, for their im-provement and diversion' acted Otway's translation of Molière's farce, *The Cheats of Scapin*. Ramsay was invited to supply a prologue for this show, part of which reads as follows:

2

Allan Ramsay: a chalk drawing by his son
Courtesy of the Scottish National Portrait Gallery

Somebody says to some fowk, we're to blame;
That 'tis a scandal and a black, burning shame
To thole young callands thus to grow sae snack
and lear—O mighty crimes!—to speak and act!
'Stage plays,' quoth Dunce, 'are unco things indeed!'
He said, he gloom'd and shook his thick boss head.
...in spite of ilk endeavour
We'll cherish wit and scorn their fead and favour;
We'll strive to bring in active eloquence,
tho, for a while, upon our fame's expense...
Knock down the fools, who dare with empty rage
spit in the face of virtue and the stage.

Although there is an element of challenge in these lines—indicating quite clearly the degree of opposition to dramatic entertainment that prevailed, not only in Edinburgh but throughout British society at that time—there is no evidence of anything more than good-natured support on Ramsay's part. Over the next few years, however, his interest in theatre increased considerably, probably due to his friendship with the actor Tony Aston.

Aston, an Irishman who also appeared under the name of 'Matt Medley', was a typical 'strolling player' of the period; the leader of a species of theatre company that was common throughout Europe for almost three centuries. Yvonne Ffrench, in her excellent biography *Mrs Siddons* (Derek Verschoyle, 1936) provides a description of this kind of company that fits Aston more or less exactly.

> Under the constant threat of indictment and always in the shadow of persecution, the strollers maintained a code of laws that had barely altered since Elizabethan times. The manager of a company was usually the member who possessed enough capital to fit the rest out with dresses and provide some meagre scenery. After expenses had been deducted the profits were divided into shares, one to each member of the troupe, and four 'dead' shares allowed to the manager in consideration of the properties. As his whole family was marshalled into the players' list he usually raked in half the profits.

Aston's appearances at Charleston and New York in 1703 are believed to have been the first by a professional actor in the Americas. For almost 50 years, he travelled all over the English-speaking world, usually in productions of his own plays, *The Fool's Opera, Love in a Hurry* and *The Coy Shepherdess*, performed mostly by himself and members of his large family. Although his comedies have not stood the test of time, it may well have been Aston's influence that was responsible for Ramsay writing his own masterpiece, *The Gentle Shepherd*.

Aston first came to Edinburgh in the early 1720s. The exact date is not known, but it could not have been later than 1725—significantly, the year in which *The Gentle Shepherd* was first published—because, in a prologue that Ramsay wrote for Aston in 1726, he refers to his friend's appearance in the previous year. It is possible, however, that Aston's arrival in Edinburgh took place even earlier. J C Dibdin, in his *Annals of the Edinburgh Stage*, expresses the opinion that 'Aston had resided in the town for many seasons'. Whether or not Dibdin is right about this, Aston certainly seems to have resolved to make his home in Edinburgh, where he had received a warm welcome, not only from the citizenry but from the authorities too. It is a matter of recorded fact that Aston's season of 1726 took place at the direct invitation of the Provost and magistrates of the city. Since, in view of what took place later, this seems somewhat surprising, it would be as well to pause and reflect on the reason for this invitation.

The government of Edinburgh at that time fell some way short of being a true democracy. The 'ordinary' council consisted of 25 members, elected, in a complicated process, by the city's 14 trade guilds. It was this body which elected the eight magistrates who had the real power; four bailies, the Dean of Guild, the Treasurer and the Lord Provost. By far the most important of those was the Lord Provost and, in 1725, this office was held by the formidable figure of George Drummond.

Drummond, whose abundant energy and dictatorial nature was to dominate city politics in Edinburgh for the best part of 50 years, was just beginning the first of his six terms of office. (In a life that was devoted to civic improvement, he promoted the establishment of the New Town, although perhaps his greatest achievement was the creation of the Royal Infirmary, a project he actually initiated in that year of 1725.) A dedicated Hanoverian, Drummond had, at the age of just 18, been appointed Accountant-General to the Scottish Parliament and, as such, had been responsible for the financial computations involved in the negotiations of the Act of Union in 1707. In 1715, he had taken up arms in opposition to the Earl of Mar's unsuccessful rebellion and, 30 years later, he would become responsible for the defence of Edinburgh against the advancing army of Prince Charles Edward Stuart. He was a man, in short, who identified the Union and the Hanoverian succession with stability and progress.

Allan Ramsay, with his Jacobite sympathies, might be thought to have had little in common with George Drummond. Yet there is some evidence to suggest that they were, at least, on good terms—Ramsay refers to the Provost as 'dear Drummond' in one of his poems—and both men would have regarded the establishment of a theatre in Edinburgh as a desirable objective, Ramsay as part of his cultural agenda, Drummond on civic grounds. In matters of civic development—although possibly for different reasons—they were certainly at one. It is equally certain that the invitation that Aston received would never have been offered without Drummond's approval and it may well have been Ramsay's influence that obtained this.

Ramsay promoted Aston's activities in several ways: by writing prologues for his performances, by selling tickets at his bookshop and, most interestingly, by publishing a pamphlet, *Some Hints in Defence of Dramatic Entertainment* (1727), which reads at times like a glowing testimonial to Aston's character.

> Mr Aston and his family live themselves, to my certain knowledge, with sobriety, justice and discretion: he pays his debts without being dunn'd; is of a charitable disposition and avoids the intoxicating bottle.

One argument frequently used against the theatre by its enemies was that the profits made by visiting companies was money lost to the city, since it was inevitably spent elsewhere. Ramsay dealt with this objection in his pamphlet, firstly by pointing out that the visiting players incurred a great deal of expenditure while they were in the city and, secondly, by pointing out that 'Mr Aston is resolved to live and die in this place'.

Ramsay's defence of Aston had become necessary, not because of any serious public outcry, but simply because of action taken by the office of Thomas Johns, Master of the Revels in Scotland. This official, a member of the Royal Household, acted as the sovereign's deputy in all matters pertaining to public entertainment at that time: licensing plays, companies, playhouses built on Crown land, hearing complaints and levying fines. Dues paid to the Revels Office formed part of the necessary expense of every theatrical production. At the commencement of Aston's 1726 season, the Revels office denied him a licence to perform.

Exactly why this action was taken can only be guessed at. It can hardly have been a matter of the nature of Aston's performances, since he had been presenting the same programme for the best part of 20 years. It is possible that someone had made a complaint about him but, if so, this did not appear in the citation that the Master brought before the city magistrates. A much more likely explanation is that Aston, thinking he had the support of these magistrates—in a late court hearing, he would also produce evidence of the support of the Earl of Lauderdale, Lord Belhaven and Lord Somerset—had defied the Revels office by witholding the dues that the Master required him to pay. If this was indeed the case, it was a serious mistake on Aston's part.

When Aston tried to open his 1727 season, he found that the patronage of the previous year had been withdrawn and that he was now prohibited from playing in Edinburgh. This *volte face* on the part of Edinburgh's magistracy can only be explained by Aston's defiance of the Revels office. (Dibdin, in his *Annals*, draws attention to the fact that the government of the city had changed by this time, but there can surely be little significance in that. It is true that Drummond had demitted the office of Lord Provost in favour of one John Macauley, but he was still on the council and, no matter what office he held, exerted a powerful, at times dictatorial, influence over the city's affairs.) In matters pertaining to the theatre, the city magistrates were always concerned, as we shall shortly see, to act within the letter of the law.

Undeterred by the prohibition, Aston opened with his comedy *Love for Love* and announced another play for production. The magistrates immediately fined him for contempt, charged him not to 'act any play, farce or comedy' and even ordered that the Skinner's Hall, where Aston had been playing, be locked up against him. Aston, who seems to have had some legal training, was not prepared to take this lying down and immediately raised a bill of suspension in the Court of Session, challenging the right of the new council to withdraw his patronage. Despite every argument to the contrary, the Lords of Session granted Aston his bill and allowed him to continue producing his plays.

These bare facts, however, give little indication of the high emotions that were raised by this case or the root cause of the disfavour into which Aston had fallen. *Mist's Weekly Journal* of December, 1727, casts an interesting sidelight on the affair.

> Last Sunday the Kirk pulpits were thump'd in a violent and outragious manner, and the case of abominations feelingly display'd with abundance of pious rhetoric on account of Tony Aston's being tolerated to entertain the *beaus* and *belles* with his comick scenes and representations. The pastors had got the magistrates on their side, and had plac'd a guard of soldiers, with their bayonets on their muskets, at the door of his Theatre, to prevent the Ladies going in, and put an end to the Acting; but the matter being brought before a higher Court, where the Ladies had a pretty considerable influence, the prohibition was taken off and Tony restor'd to his privilege of diverting the Town, as well as the more serious Drolls.

This article prompts a couple of interesting questions. Who, for instance, were those 'ladies' who had to be prevented from entering the theatre at the point of fixed bayonets, and who seem to have had an inordinate influence over the justiciary? They were, no doubt, the wives and sisters of judges, such as Lady Elliot of Minto and Mrs Brown of Coalstoun, both active during this period in helping the Hon. Miss Nicky Murray (sister of the Earl of Mansfield) to organise dances in Assembly Close. Twenty years later, they (or their counterparts) would swoon over the person of Prince Charles Edward Stuart, in spite of the opposition of their husbands and brothers.

A rather more important question concerns the attitude of the ministers. In Edinburgh at that time (as in the rest of the country) the Church of Scotland reigned supreme and there were few other denominations: a United Presbyterian meeting-house in Bristo, an Episcopalian chapel in Blackfriars Wynd, very few Catholics and no Jews. In all matters relating to Scottish Theatre history, the opposition of the Kirk is taken so much for granted that the grounds on which it was based are rarely discussed. It is important to understand, however, that this opposition was very much part of the social climate of the time.

The Presbyterian objection to the theatre was not a matter of politics or morals, but was made on philosophical and theological grounds. It related not only to the condition of the theatre at any given time, but to the very act of theatre itself. A hundred years after the Tony Aston case, at a time when the theatre was beginning to enjoy a degree of respectability, an Edinburgh minister, the Rev. John Macdonald published a pamphlet, entitled *What is the Theatre?*, which summed up the Presbyterian attitude in the following terms:

> The theatre, existing as it does, by the preponderance of evil, must of necessity *continue to be evil*—so that its principle of vitality is evil…We admit that there is good mixed up with it…It is the little good that is in it that makes its evil nature so dangerous; it is the decent character of a few actors that obtains social toleration for the many; it is the comparative morality of some plays that forms an ideal protection for the rest. But the evil is evil still…and so long as the stage lives by evil, it must itself be necessarily and essentially evil. Even as Christ hath said, 'Do men gather grapes of thorns, or figs of thistles? A good tree cannot bring forth evil fruit; *neither can a corrupt tree bring forth good fruit.*

Now this was an argument to which it was not, of course, possible for the theatre to adjust. It created tremendous difficulty, particularly when one considers the preponderance of Presbyterian influence. There were, in all, nine churches in Edinburgh at this time, and each of them had two ministers. Since they had, according to Presbyterian practice, been called—that is to say, elected—by their congregations, they were more representative of the people than the councillors, who owed their positions largely to their wealth. Moreover, these ministers were all of a character which was at the furthest remove from the gentle and civilized occupants of the pulpits of today. The religious persecutions of the seventeenth century were still within reach of living memory and they had all been brought up in the fighting tradition of the Covenanters. Even the most forward-looking and sympathetic of the magistrates—including Drummond and Patrick Lindsay, who became Lord Provost in 1729—knew that their views had to be treated with the utmost care.

7

It soon became clear, therefore, that while Tony Aston might have won a battle, he was bound to lose the war. A few days after his bill of suspension was granted, Aston was summoned to appear before the magistrates as a result of a petition raised by Lady Morrison, his neighbour in Skinner's Close, who claimed that Aston's business was damaging her house. Large numbers of people, it was claimed, 'bended' Lady Morison's roof to the extent that 'the house was in danger in being destroyed by the fall of the floor.'

No fewer than 15 skilled tradesmen—members of the guilds who, it will be recalled, elected the 'ordinary' members of the Town Council—testified that Lady Morrison's house was in an unsafe condition and, as a result of this, the earlier decision in favour of Aston was reversed.

Thus began a series of appeals and counter-appeals by Aston and the magistrates to the Lords of Session, a lengthy and contentious legal battle, the details of which need not detain us. There could only be one outcome in this unequal struggle and, at some point in the proceedings, Tony Aston must have realised this. In the spring of 1728, he decided to cut his losses and leave Edinburgh forever.

As for Allan Ramsay, if he felt disheartened by the experience of his friend, his spirits were soon to be raised. Six months later, in October 1728, a new company arrived in the city, took a lease on a piece of ground in the Canongate and announced their intention to erect a playhouse. This company, the Edinburgh Company of Players, was to remain in the city for the next seven years. Although their intended playhouse was never built—the site may have been that used 20 years later for the Canongate Theatre—they played regular seasons at the Taylor's Hall in the Cowgate and toured extensively throughout Scotland, visiting Montrose, Dundee, and Aberdeen. Their endeavours met with a great deal of success and, more importantly, no opposition whatsoever. Throughout their stay in Edinburgh, the company never had the least difficulty with either the magistrates or the Church.

There were a number of reasons for this. First, unlike Tony Aston's company, the Edinburgh Players were in possession of a Royal Patent. This meant, in effect, that no-one had the right to impede their activities and that they were more or less independent of the civil authorities. (As far as the Church was concerned, ministers might continue to thump their pulpits, but they were Hanoverians to a man and would think more than twice before going against His Majesty's pleasure.) Secondly, the new company seems to have made some important local connections.

The *Caledonian Mercury* of 4 June, 1733, contains the announcement of a benefit of John Gay's *The Beggar's Opera* to be given in aid of the Edinburgh Infirmary 'the whole profits from that night's performance to be given to the managers of that hospital without the least drawback.' Since, as we have seen, the creation of the Infirmary was George Drummond's most favoured project, it is clear from this that the Edinburgh Players had won the support of the most powerful man in the city.

Other powerful influences were also at work. Seven years later, in the January of 1735, the *Caledonian Mercury* carried the following notice.

> Yesternight the several members of the Most Ancient and Honourable Society of Free Masons now here, march'd in procession with aprons and white gloves, attended with flambeaux, to the play-house, Taylor's Hall, where they saw (acted at their desire) the comedy of *Henry the Fourth*.

Quite clearly, the Edinburgh Players enjoyed a high degree of social acceptance, which rather put any enemies they may have had at a disadvantage. To be absolutely fair, however, to the citizens of Edinburgh and to the company itself, this social acceptance does seem to have been wholly justified.

The quality of drama that the Edinburgh Players presented was far superior to that of Tony Aston. In place of farce and low comedy, there was Shakespeare (albeit the corrupted Shakespeare of Davenant, Dryden and Nahum Tate), Molière, Vanburgh, John Gay and Henry Fielding. As far as the standard of acting is concerned, this can only be guessed at, but the indications are that it was of a very high order indeed. John Ware, who managed the company, later became an associate of John Rich of the newly-opened Covent Garden Theatre in London—it may have been this connection that secured the Royal Patent in the first place—and the original company included two actors who would later make their mark on the English stage: Harry Woodward and James Quin.

Allan Ramsay's relationship with the Edinburgh Players was obviously very close, although not, perhaps, as amicable as his relationship with Tony Aston had been. Apart from providing his support as a leading Edinburgh citizen—not to mention the service of his bookshop as a ticket agency—Ramsay himself was achieving a degree of theatrical success at this time. In 1729, music was added to *The Gentle Shepherd* and it was presented as a ballad opera by the boys of Haddington Grammar School in the Taylor's Hall. The success of this production—the first of many the play has enjoyed over the centuries—led to a London production (in an English translation by Theophilus Cibber) at Drury Lane.

What with the established success of the Edinburgh Players, Ramsay's emergence as a dramatist and the plans for a new play-house in the Canongate, conditions seemed right for the establishment of Edinburgh as a regular theatrical centre. Then, in 1736, for some reason—about which existing records are absolutely silent—the Edinburgh Players lost their Royal Patent and decided to disband.

It was for this reason that Allan Ramsay opened his theatre in Carrubber's Close. This enterprise therefore was not, as has often been suggested, a new initiative but rather an attempt to carry through a project that Ramsay and others had been working on for the past seven years.

> The new theatre in Carrubber's Close, being in great forwardness, will be opened the first of November. These are to advertise the Gentlemen and Ladies who incline to

purchase Annual Tickets, to enter their names before the Twentieth of October next, on which day they shall receive their tickets from Allan Ramsay on paying 30s. No more than forty to be subscribed for. After which none will be disposed of under two guineas.

Now, when the above notice appeared in the *Caledonian Mercury* on 16 September, 1736, Allan Ramsay could not have been aware that he was opening a theatre which would face closure in little more than six months time. He invested a great deal of money in fitting up Carrubber's Close and employing a company of actors. From the single cast list that survives, it is clear that this company was made up of former members of the Edinburgh Company of Players. The theatre opened on 8 November, 1736, with a production of George Farquhar's comedy, *The Recruiting Officer*.

The story of how this theatre came to grief contains some interesting sidelights. For several years past, the Prime Minister, Robert Walpole, irritated by the constant attacks on his government by Henry Fielding and other playwrights, had been eager to introduce legislation that would regulate the licensing of plays. According to a rumour that was current at the time, he engineered this by employing some anonymous hack to write a scurrilous play of pronounced Jacobite sympathies, entitled *The Golden Rump*. This was submitted for production at the Goodman's Fields Theatre under the name of Henry Fielding. The manager of Goodman's Fields, Henry Giffard, took the play to Walpole, who immediately showed the piece to the King and secured permission to introduce his Theatres Act. Giffard, it was said, was rewarded with the sum of £1,000 in compensation for the loss of his business.

The Theatres Act gave a monopoly of legitimate theatrical production to just two theatres: Covent Garden and Drury Lane. Both of these, of course, were in London and as far as the provinces, including Scotland, were concerned, no performance could be given that did not have a licence from the Lord Chamberlain.

By the following June, then, Carrubber's Close had become illegal and Ramsay was required to close down. In an rhymed address to Forbes of Culloden, Lord President of the Session—of which the following is an extract—Ramsay protested against this requirement and made a request that he either be allowed to remain open until the debts of the theatre were cleared, or else be re-imbursed from the public funds.

> Is there ought better than the stage
> To mend the follies of the age,
> If managed as it ought to be,
> Frae ilka vice and blaidry free?
> Which may be done with perfect ease,
> And nought be heard that shall displease,
> Or give the least offense or pain
> If we can hae't restored again.

> Wherefore, my lords, I humbly pray
> Our lads may be allowed to play,
> At least till new-house debts be paid off,
> The cause that I'm the maist afraid of;
> Which load lies on my single back
> And I may pay it, ilka plack.

Neither request was granted and Ramsay was obliged to bear the loss himself. For many years, it was believed that Ramsay, according to Dibdin, 'quietly submitted and discontinued his connection with actors and acting'.

Recent research, however, has revealed that this was not the case. Ramsay may have closed down in June, but the theatre was open again the following winter, when a ballad opera by a young Edinburgh writer called Adam Thomson was produced. The printed version of this play, entitled *Buckram in Armour*, appeared in 1738. The title page of this volume gives details of a performance which took place on the previous winter, making it perfectly clear that Carrubber's Close was functioning in the winter of 1737.

There can be no doubt either that Ramsay was still in charge. In August of 1738, he wrote to his friend, the Hon. John Murray, in terms that clearly indicate that his 'connection with actors and acting' had not been discontinued.

> I find it will be something difficult with me at first to get a company up to my mind, but I'll make the best shift I can. I am desir'd by some to let the whole troop at Newcastle (who are now in Scarborough) come here at once, and I begin to think that it will not be amiss to let all come that incline for the first season.

The 'whole troop' to which this letter refers is presumably the company that had previously been acting at Carrubber's Close. It did however, have one interesting addition: the leading actor of this company was none other than that same Henry Giffard who had been manipulated by Walpole into providing the ammunition for the Theatres Act! In the January of 1739, one John Morrison was arrested for putting up placards for a production of Colley Cibber's *The Careless Husband* at Carrubber's Close theatre. According to *Scoto-Dramatica Fragmentica* (ed. James Maidment, Edinburgh, 1851) Morrison was in Giffard's employment. These placards carried the arms of Scotland and the truculent motto *Nemo Me Impune Lacessit*, giving the strongest indication that both men were acting at the behest of Allan Ramsay. Giffard's association with Ramsay at this time would tend to exonerate him from the charge of having betrayed his calling for Walpole's gold—unless, of course, Walpole renegued on the deal—and, furthermore, since Giffard had been one of the most successful actor-managers of his time, it gives a strong indication of the level of Ramsay's ambition. That ambition, however, was soon to be thwarted.

On the Wednesday after Morrison's arrest, the Edinburgh Presbytery met and instructed its agent, Mr Spence, to lay a complaint before the City Council. As a result of this, the theatre was raided by a party of the City Guard, under the command of the Town Officer, William Scot.

On entering the theatre, Scot was immediately challenged by a member of the audience, a lawyer called Samuel Mariot, who demanded to see Scot's warrant. This proved to be null because, although it listed a number of people to be arrested, it was not signed. In spite of this, Scot insisted on carrying out his orders, which rather enraged Mariot. Producing what were later described as 'instruments' (possibly pistols) he called Scot and his men 'scoundrels' and declared that, if they did not leave immediately, he would 'throw 'em over the window and break their necks'.

Mariot's outburst led to his immediate arrest—he was later bound over to keep the peace and fined five pounds—but it did create enough of a diversion for the members of the company to escape. They left the jurisdiction of Edinburgh by the Netherbow port and took refuge in the Holyrood Sanctuary, where they remained in hiding for several weeks, until the case was heard before the Court of Session. On 2 March, 1739, despite a brilliant defence by Henry Home, the future Lord Kames, each member of the company was fined £50, to be levied by distress or sale of goods, the alternative being three months imprisonment. Before this conviction could be enforced, however, the actors had fled the city.

As far as Ramsay himself was concerned, no action was taken, in spite of a demand by the Presbytery that he be charged with running an illegal theatre. The City magistrates were not about to put Scotland's leading poet in jail. Besides, Ramsay had some very powerful friends and, even as his actors were fleeing the city, he was planning his next move. As a matter of fact, he seems to have maintained an attitude of supreme confidence throughout this whole affair. A fortnight after the raid by Scot, for example, he told John Murray that he would arrange for the actors to have extra benefits to defray the expense of the trial.

This confidence was far from being misplaced. Under the terms of the Theatres Act, it was impossible for any theatre to remain legally in business without either a licence from the Lord Chamberlain or Letters Patent from the Monarch. While Allan Ramsay was of course in possession of neither, this does not mean that he had no hopes of procuring some kind of legal status. Even as Ramsay's actors lay in hiding, moves were taking place in London that promised the fulfilment of such hopes.

Lord Glenorchy, MP for Saltash, supporter and confidant of Walpole, had agreed to place a Bill before the House of Commons, enabling the Lord Chamberlain to license a theatre in Edinburgh. All that was required was a list of possible patentees, to be supplied by John Murray, who seems to have been associated with Ramsay in this venture. Glenorchy, in a letter to Murray, hinted that Ramsay's name should not be on this list, but otherwise expressed his confidence that the measure would be carried.

When the Provost and bailies were informed of Glenorchy's Bill, they reacted with extreme hostility. Patrick Lindsay, now Member of Parliament for Edinburgh, was instructed to 'use every lawfull means to him that shall appear fit in behalf of the city' and this instruction was accompanied by three separate petitions against Glenorchy's Bill: one from the Council, one from the Dean of Guild and a long list of citizens, and one from the University. Faced with such opposition, it is little wonder that Glenorchy withdrew the measure. In a speech to the Commons, he declared that

> Since the people of Edinburgh shew by these petitions a disposition to submit to their chains, I have no objection to their wearing them and will therefore trouble the House no further upon this subject.

Nothwithstanding previous disputes, the vigour and intensity of opposition contained in these petitions may seem somewhat surprising. It is one thing to prosecute law-breakers—as, in the case of the Carrubber's Close company, the magistrates were obliged to do—but quite another to take such swift and decisive action against a perfectly reasonable attempt to change the law. After all, the Edinburgh Company of Players, a legal company, had flourished in the city for seven years prior to 1735, without any objection whatsoever. Glenorchy's Bill proposed nothing more than restoring this situation.

In order to understand the attitude of the Edinburgh petitioners, however, it is necessary to return to the Aston case in 1727. Charles Erskine of Tinwald, acting for the magistrates, made an address to the court, part of which reads as follows:

> Order and good government require that not only crimes, but whatsoever else may disturb the public tranquility or be noxious to it, should be represt...how innocent so ever public diversions may be, they are certainly the occasion of drawing great assemblies together, and for that reason have always been considered as of very great consequence to any populous place.

That was in 1727. Ten years later, in the September of 1737—three months after Carrubber's Close had become illegal—an event took place in the city that was considerably more dramatic than anything that could possibly be seen on the Edinburgh stage.

In the March of 1736, a convicted smuggler called Andrew Wilson was put to death in the Grassmarket. Wilson had been a popular figure, partly because smuggling was not really considered a crime—duty on spirits was one consequence of the Act of Union which proved highly unpopular in Scotland—and partly because of his heroic part in the escape of his fellow-accused, a young man called George Robertson, on the Sunday previous to the execution. After Wilson had been despatched on the gallows, some boys in the crowd began to pelt the City Guard with dirt and stones, prompting the commander of the Guard, Captain John Porteous, to order his men to open fire. As a result of this order, nine people were killed. Porteous was charged with murder, tried and found guilty. He was due to hang on 7 September, 1737.

At the last moment—prompted, it is said, by some judges with whom Porteous habitually played golf—Queen Caroline, then acting as regent, cancelled the execution with the issue of a pardon. The population of Edinburgh, incensed by this injustice, ran riot, broke into the Tolbooth prison (where Porteous was still being held) dragged Porteous out and carried out the hanging themselves.

Queen Caroline, when she heard of this, was furious and threatened that this event would have dire consequences for the city of Edinburgh. She summoned the Provost, Alexander Wilson, to London, stripped him of his office and flung him in jail. She proposed pulling down the city walls and abolishing the Edinburgh City Guard, saying that she would turn all Scotland into 'a hunting field'.

Mercifully for Edinburgh, Queen Caroline died before her threats could be carried out. As a result of this, the penalties were substantially watered down; Alexander Wilson, although released, was banned for life from holding public office, and the city was ordered to pay a substantial pension to the widow of John Porteous. It had, however, been a near thing; if Queen Caroline had had her way, the city of Edinburgh would, at the very least, have lost many of her ancient privileges. When one further considers that the Porteous Riot was believed not to have been a spontaneous affair, but one which had been organised by a group of dissidents, one can hardly blame the authorities for being chary of 'assemblies of many persons in one body' in Carrubber's Close or anywhere else.

It was the Porteous Riot, rather than any Calvinist prejudice or civic disapproval, that led to the final defeat of the ambitions of Allan Ramsay's theatre. As a direct result, theatre in Scotland became marginalized, a social entertainment that was the preserve of the select few. Since, in a country the size of Scotland, these were very few indeed, the theatre could only survive in conditions of extreme difficulty. It would be another 27 years before a patent was granted to any Edinburgh theatre—and, even then, it was only partial, giving control of performances to the Provost and the bailies—and almost 50 years before a fully legal theatre could operate anywhere in Scotland. By that time, much damage had been done.

As far as Allan Ramsay was concerned, he retired from all business shortly after the failure of the Glenorchy Bill, and concentrated his energies in building Goosepie Lodge. He lived the last 18 years of his life as a man of leisure, surrounded by his family, his friends and his books, and if he had any further connection with theatrical affairs, there is no record of it. Considering that so much effort and expense had yielded almost nothing in return, it is likely that he was sick and tired of the whole business.

At the same time, one cannot be sure of this. In the September of 1741, an announcement appeared in the *Caledonian Mercury* which might well have brought a smile to Honest Allan's face.

> By particular desire of a Lady of Quality, for the benefit of Mrs Hamilton, on Monday next, being the 31st instant, at the Taylor's Hall, in the Cowgate, will be given a Concert of Vocal and Instrumental Musick. After which, will be given, gratis, *The Mourning Bride*, after which will be added, gratis, *The Toy Shop*. Entertainments between the acts by Mr and Mrs Millar.

Mrs Hamilton was Henry Giffard's sister-in-law and, together with the Millers, Giffard and her husband, had been in the Holyrood Sanctuary three years earlier. They were all perfectly well aware of the penalties that the law could exact. It was not, however, against the law to give free performances for one's friends and if, in order to take advantage of this, it was necessary for the audience to buy a ticket for a concert, that was perfectly legal too.

By this and other measures, the provisions of the Theatres Act were circumvented over the years. Although it would remain in force for more than a hundred years, Walpole's legislation—a petty-minded measure, born out of personal pique—was to prove to be cumbersome to administer and so became increasingly unworkable. The time would come, as we shall see, when even a successful prosecution under the Act could be safely ignored. As far as Scotland was concerned, however, its main effect was to inhibit theatrical development—and this would be case for as long as it remained on the statute book.

Chapter Two

THE SCOTTISH ROSCIUS

Despite its Edinburgh location and the cultural ambitions of its owner, the Carrubber's Close Theatre was never a particularly Scottish institution. As far as can be established, only three of Ramsay's actors were Scottish—one Alexander Thomson and a couple called Weir—and all the others came from London. Furthermore, the only Scottish play that the company is known for certain to have produced—assuming, in the absence of any evidence to the contrary, that there was no production of *The Gentle Shepherd*—was Adam Thomson's *Buckram in Armour*, a ballad opera very much in the fashionable style of John Gay, albeit with an Edinburgh setting.

On the other hand, a number of these English actors, despite the difficulties, liked Scotland well enough to remain in the country. In the setting of a legal theatre, where such talents could achieve wider public recognition, these actors might easily have stimulated a more native approach to the drama. As far as writing was concerned, the success of *Buckram in Armour* certainly should have encouraged the youthful Adam Thomson—who was only 15 years old when he wrote the play—to develop as a playwright, setting an example for others to follow.

In the long term, the most important single effect of the failure of the Glenorchy Bill proved to be the stifling of any such indigenous development. Unlicensed performances, of the kind described at the end of the last chapter, attracted audiences who were decidedly unadventurous in taste. In his withdrawal speech in the House of Commons, Glenorchy himself hinted at the ambitions of this audience.

> I told the House the Reasons that had induced me to bring in the Bill. That I did it at the desire of several Persons of Quality and Gentlemen of distinction. That I thought it an advantage to all Scotland, because 'twould introduce the English Language, which would be a benefit even to the gentlemen of this age, but more so to their posterity

who would hereafter represent that part of the Kingdom. That I looked upon it so evidently an advantage to the City of Edinburgh that 'twas impossible to imagine they could be so blind as not to see it.

The remark regarding the introduction of the 'English language' requires some explanation. Hanoverian Scotland, having accepted the Act of Union, was totally committed to the concept of Britishness and, as result, became absolutely neurotic about mode of speech. These Hanoverians looked to the theatre to provide them with examples of the current London usage and, throughout the eighteenth century, actors found that they could supplement their income while in Edinburgh by teaching English idiom and pronunciation to the Scottish bourgeoisie.

This attitude proved injurious to the theatre in two ways. First, it meant that that part of the potential audience which did not accept the Union—or, at least, accepted it only grudgingly—came to regard the theatre as an anglicizing influence and refused to have anything to do with it. Secondly, since the audience which continued to support the theatre would tolerate nothing that did not come from London, it delayed the evolution of a distinctively Scottish style for the best part of a century.

Now, the suggestion here is not that the licensing of Carrubber's Close would have created such a style overnight. The very least that can be said, however, is that the passage of the Glenorchy Bill would have created a theatrical forum in which these essentially political attitudes would have been transcended.

As it was, the organisers of unlicensed performances had no choice but to pander to the prejudices of the only audience available: the Hanoverian audience who wished to learn 'the English language'. Even these audiences, however, were not to remain satisfied for long with second-hand productions of the latest London theatrical fare. They began to hanker after a drama of their own, a truly 'British' drama which would reflect Scotland's place in the Union. In December, 1756, this demand was partially met with the first production of the most extraordinary Scottish play of them all: John Home's *Douglas*.

Before dealing with the history of *Douglas*, it would be as well to say something about the nature of theatrical production at this time. In the second half of the eighteenth century, this was in a very primitive state. Lighting was used simply for illumination—with no attempt to suggest atmosphere—and set design usually did no more than give the merest suggestion of the dramatic environment. Actors usually performed all plays, including Shakespeare and the classics, in contemporary dress. Although costume sometimes gave some indication of character—Macbeth, for instance, was often played in the uniform of a general in the British Army— there was absolutely no interest in authenticity. Acting itself was largely a matter of recitation—or, to be more accurate, declamation—and ensemble playing was more or less unknown. Leading players would usually study in solitude and the finished production would be put together in one or two rehearsals.

As far as dramatists were concerned, Walpole's Theatres Act had driven the best of them from the stage. Plays continued to be written, of course, but they had to be tailored to the needs of the leading actors—handsome and athletic men, magnificently beautiful women—whose dominating presence reigned supreme. When one thinks of eighteenth century English theatre, one does not think of Rowe or Otway or Holcroft, but of David Garrick, John Philip Kemble, Peg Woffington and Mrs Siddons.

It is in this context that *Douglas* must be judged. In terms of dramatic effect, its popularity did not long outlast its time. ('The play has been quite dead for many years;' wrote James Dibdin in 1888, 'but it is, perhaps, worthy of perusal if only to see what stuff went down with our forefathers for work of genius.') Yet there is no doubting the sensation *Douglas* created on its first appearance. This sensation is perhaps best exemplified by the famous anecdote of an anonymous first-nighter who, at some point during the second act, called out enthusiastically 'Whaur's yer Wully Shakespeare nou?'

Whoever he was, that first-nighter was not alone in his enthusiasm. The play won many ecstatic supporters, including such luminaries of the Scottish Enlightenment as David Hume, Henry Mackenzie and Adam Smith.

> The play had unbounded success for a great many nights in Edinburgh, and was attended by all the literati and most of the judges, who, except one or two, had not been in use to attend the theatre. The town in general was in an uproar of exultation that a Scotchman had written a tragedy of the first rate, and that its merit was first submitted to their judgement.

So wrote Dr Alexander Carlyle of Inveresk, one of the play's most enthusiastic champions and close friend of the author, John Home. That first production took place in the Canongate Theatre (whose history will form the background to a later chapter) when the part of the hero, Young Norval, was taken by the actor-manager, West Digges.

In 1757, *Douglas* opened at Covent Garden with the Irish actor, Spranger Barry, as Young Norval and Peg Woffington as Lady Randolph. Over the next 50 years, the play was revived many times and the part of Young Norval became a favoured vehicle for many of the leading actors of the day. From the point of view of this history, however, the most interesting Young Norval of all was Henry Erskine Johnston, whose performances earned him the title of 'The Scottish Roscius'.

Harry Johnston was the first Scottish actor to make more than a passing impression on his audience, the first real star of the Scottish stage. He was born in May, 1777, in Edinburgh, but seems to have spent at least part of his childhood in London. In 1794, however, he was certainly in Edinburgh, where he was serving his time as an apprentice to a linen-draper.

At this time, Johnston was 17 years old, tall, handsome and athletic. He had received no dramatic training and—apart from some amateur performances as a child—had no experience of the stage whatsoever. He did, however, have a natural aptitude for mimicry, particularly mimicry of gesture. As a party trick, he would often amuse his friends by taking off the mannerisms of famous actors, describing how each of them would play the character of Harlequin. (On one such occasion, apparently, this routine had a spectacular ending. In imitating the famous mime, Bologna—who ended his act with a great leap—Johnston leapt clean through a second-floor window and landed in the garden, 16 feet below!) He also had a certain talent, it seems, for reciting verse.

One is tempted to imagine that some astute theatrical might have spotted his talent at some social gathering and offered to help him make his way on the stage, but the truth is probably much more mundane.

Despite his humble-sounding occupation, Johnston came from a social background that was no means lowly. As the godson of Lord Thomas Erskine—a Scot who had migrated to England and found fame, fortune and political influence at the English Bar—he had access to spheres of high social status and financial resource. He first appearance in Edinburgh was, quite clearly, a conscious attempt to launch a theatrical career.

This performance took place in a building which will later loom large in our story. The Theatre Royal, Shakespeare Square—whose colourful history will be explored in the next two chapters—opened its doors for the first time on 9 December, 1769. It was originally brought into being as part of the urban planning that created Edinburgh's New Town and, for the next 90 years, would hold its place as Scotland's leading playhouse. It was, moreover, completely legal, being in possession of a Royal Patent. It was originally built, with the backing of an Edinburgh cartel, by David Ross, an actor whose considerable talents were betrayed by a feckless lifestyle—his contemporary, the actor-manager Tate Wilkinson, used to call him 'the prince of negligence'—and who squandered the great opportunities that the New Town presented, more or less running the theatre into the ground. It was purchased from Ross by John Jackson in 1781, whose ten years of management ended in bankruptcy in 1791. By the time of Johnston's debut, Jackson had sold the theatre to the management of Stephen Kemble, the manager who gave Harry Johnston his first opportunity.

Since this first appearance was entirely unannounced, it is fair to assume that either Johnston or, more likely, someone acting on his behalf, had simply hired the theatre for this purpose. The part he selected for his debut was that of the Prince in *Hamlet*: a typically impulsive gesture from a 17-year-old, but one that was to pay off handsomely.

The next day, Stephen Kemble placed the following notice in the *Edinburgh Courant*:

> Mr Kemble does himself the honour of informing the nobility and public at large that the YOUNG GENTLEMAN who performed Hamlet with so much credit to himself and satisfaction to the public, has kindly offered to assist the Theatre tomorrow evening, by which means ladies and gentlemen who were disappointed of seeing the wonderful talents of this self-taught actor—this northern luminary of the stage—may be gratified; Therefore tomorrow, Friday, June 11th, will be acted Hamlet. Hamlet—the Young Gentleman; Ghost—Woods; Ophelia—Miss Poole.

Henry Erskine Johnston as Douglas by Henry Singleton
Courtesy of the Garrick Club

Johnston played a few nights more before taking his benefit on 23 June—and it was on that evening that he first appeared as Young Norval in *Douglas*, giving for the first time the performance which made him famous.

Now, the Scottish dimension of *Douglas* not being particularly prominent, actors had previously tried to give this greater emphasis by dressing Young Norval in a tweed jacket and tartan trews. This was how the audience expected to see Johnston and there was a gasp of astonishment—followed by a loud and spontaneous burst of applause—when he stepped on to the stage in the full ensemble of a Highland chieftain: in kilt, plaid, breastplate, bonnet, shield and claymore.

John Home, the author of *Douglas*, was present on that occasion and, at the end of the evening, pronounced Johnston the *beau-ideal* of his conception, a remark we need not take too seriously. (He paid the same compliment to the child prodigy Master Betty some years later, and probably said something similar to every actor he saw in the rôle.) Yet there can be no doubting the importance of that evening as far as Johnston was concerned. For the rest of his career, he was to be indentified with the rôle of Young Norval.

At the time, of course, this was all very much in the future and young Johnston was probably a little blasé about his success, since he was concentrating on a quite different matter. Not far from the Theatre Royal, there was another place of entertainment which was to figure prominently in Johnston's life. This theatre, situated at the head of Leith Walk, was to have a plethora of names—Royal Circus, the Pantheon and New Sadler's Wells are just three of them—and a variety of uses. At the time, it was known as the Edinburgh Equestrian Circus and operated as a riding school, assembly room and concert hall. One of the riding instructors was an Irishman called Parker, whose pretty young daughter Nanette was one of the dancers in the ballet.

Where and when Johnston and Nanette first met is not known, but there is no doubt that he had fallen deeply in love with her. Every night when he was not appearing at the Theatre Royal, he would go to the Circus to watch her dance and would always throw a bouquet of flowers on the stage at the conclusion of her performance. His feelings were reciprocated and, in spite of their youth—she was just 15 years old while he himself, of course, was only two years older—they were married later that year. It was a happy and successful marriage, which would last almost 20 years, producing six children. Ten years later, Nanette was to become the unwitting cause of the most sensational episode in Johnston's life.

For the next three years, however, the Johnstons remained in Edinburgh, apart from a number of Irish engagements, in Belfast, Dublin and Cork. Then, in 1797, Johnston took his tartans to London, making his first appearance—as Young Norval, of course—at Covent Garden on 23 October, 1797. His success in London was as immediate as it had been in Edinburgh and he was praised in the *European Review* for 'figure, countenance and voice'. He remained in London for the next eight years, six of them at Covent Garden—with summer appearances at the Haymarket—during which time he played, in addition to Young Norval, Hamlet, Romeo and Petruchio, and created a number of new rôles in plays by Morton, Holcroft and Tom Dibdin. In 1803, he became involved in a dispute with the management and moved to Drury Lane for the next two years. In 1805, however, he was re-engaged by Covent Garden and in the October of that year returned to play the title rôle of Rugantino in a new play by Matthew 'Monk' Lewis, *The Bravo of Venice*. This play, like all Lewis's work, was a melodrama and, in view of what was to take place during its run, this would appear to be appropriate.

Nanette was also in the company at this time. Although there is some conflict of opinion regarding her acting—some sources describe this as 'indifferent', others praise her in particular rôles—there is absolutely no doubt about her physical beauty. By all accounts, she was an exceptionally attractive woman and, on one momentous evening, she caught the eye of the Prince of Wales.

The future George IV was a man whose best qualities were, to say the least, well-hidden and who was notorious for his love of excess. According to the diarist, Charles Greville, he spent the greater part of every day in bed and would not make the slightest exertion if he had a servant to make it on his behalf. As Heir Apparent, he had access to seemingly unlimited funds and squandered many fortunes on fine houses, jewellery, clothes, race-horses and elegant women. His love of eating, drinking, sex and every kind of extravagance was legendary. He drank brandy by the bucketful and indulged himself in dinner parties which could last as long as 12 hours. As far as sex was concerned, he had a definite penchant for pretty actresses.

As soon as he saw Nanette, the Prince decided that nothing would do but that he must make her acquaintance as soon as possible. Without even having the courtesy to wait until the performance was concluded, the Prince went backstage between the acts and forced his way into Mrs Johnston's dressing-room. Whatever improprieties took place there are scarcely to be guessed at, but the fact is that, as soon as Johnston heard of this, he flew into a furious rage. The Scottish Roscius lost no time in equipping himself with a horse-whip and seeking out the man who had insulted his wife. At the hands of Harry Johnston, the future George IV received a painful, undignified and (probably) thoroughly deserved thrashing.

Johnston was immediately put under arrest—and immediately escaped from custody. He went into hiding in a cheap boarding-house in the Borough of Lambeth, remaining there for some weeks, until the fuss surrounding the affair had blown over. Then, disguised as an old soldier, he left London and travelled north by foot, not stopping until he reached Newcastle.

Johnston was never prosecuted for his assault on the Prince, probably due to the influence of his godfather, Lord Erskine. Erskine was Lord Chancellor by this time and had, in any case, always enjoyed the Prince's confidence. He probably persuaded George to let the matter drop; it would not, after all, be in the best interests of the realm to draw public attention to the fact that the Heir Apparent had been physically humiliated by a jealous husband—especially when that husband was, of all things, an actor! Apart from this, there was an altogether more pressing problem to be considered. In 1795, the Prince had been forced into marriage to Caroline of Brunswick in order to settle a massive debt of £650,000. In an attempt to get out of this purely mercenary union—which had been blessed with a daughter, Charlotte Augusta—he had initiated the so-called 'Delicate Investigation' accusing the unhappy Caroline of adultery with the artist Thomas Lawrence. In spite of every precaution on the part of both the Prince and his advisers, the press had got hold of the story and the last thing that was needed was a scandal involving the Prince himself.

This being the case, Johnston escaped any kind of legal penalty for his act. Even so, his London career appeared to be over, obliging him to solve his problems by going into provincial management. Under a statute passed in 1788, certain 'places of resort' were permitted to operate theatres, under license from the local magistrates, for a limited season each year. These seasons, restricted to a maximum of 60 performances and a time limit of three months, led to a series of touring circuits, based on major towns. Initially, Johnston worked on the Newcastle circuit, then moved back to Scotland and, for the next few years, managed seasons at Ayr and Greenock.

He must have had some success with this because, in 1808, he put in a substantial bid for the lease of the Edinburgh Theatre Royal. His letter of application to Robert Dundas of the Theatre Royal Trustees—which still exists in the National Library of Scotland—makes rather interesting reading.

> I am the only one (of the candidates) who can boast that he is a native of this city, upon whose theatrical boards, in early life, commenced with some approbation my Dramatic career; and who, with a flattering degree of public applause, have continued these fourteen years past, a devoted performer in this line, to the theatres of London and Dublin, at which last I was lately called upon to take a considerable share of the management.
>
> I understand that a committee has been appointed by His Grace and yourself, to fix upon a proper manager. To that committee, I have communicated my terms and, if with your and their sanction, I shall be the fortunate candidate, I flatter myself that I will be found competent to render the Theatre of my native city equal to that of any in the British Empire, whose Constitution, Law and Government I not only venerate and esteem, but will use every exertion in my power to support and preserve; towards which I personally became, while in London, connected with the Regiment of Loyal North Britons, and while in Edinburgh was a member of the R.E.V.

These protestations of loyalty would appear to indicate that the scandal of his assault on the Prince of Wales was something he was anxious to live down.

His bid, however, was unsuccessful and he turned his attentions from Scotland to Ireland, investing heavily—to the tune of some £6,000—in building a new theatre in Dublin. This theatre, the Royal Hibernian, had a short and disastrous life. At the time, there were two other theatres in Dublin—Smock Alley and Crow Street—and it was soon evident that there was no room for a third. By 1812, the *Irish Dramatic Censor* was reporting that Johnston's 'private fortune, all the hard savings of a life of theatrical industry, has gone to wreck in the contest'. Privately, as well as professionally, this was a bad time for Johnston; as he struggled to pay his creditors, he was faced with the undeniable fact of his wife's infidelity to him with a succession of lovers. He added to the burden of his debts by initiating a divorce suit and when, two years later, this was granted, he left Dublin forever. He returned to Scotland, where he was engaged as manager of the Queen Street Theatre Royal in Glasgow.

In 1814, the great period of industrial development, when Glasgow became the 'Second City of the British Empire', was only just beginning. Glasgow, then, was a bustling commercial centre, best known for its tobacco trade with America—which was just coming to an end—and its burgeoning shipping business. After almost a century of difficulty—to be explored in a later chapter—theatre in Glasgow was at last becoming established. The playhouse that Johnston was given to manage was a splendid affair, built at the cost of £18,500 and billed as 'the most magnificent Provincial Theatre in the Empire'.

It might have been the beginning of a glorious chapter in the history of the Scottish theatre. Like its namesake in Edinburgh, the Glasgow Theatre Royal held a Royal Patent and was completely legal. Although his own appearances had been rare over the last ten years, Johnston was still famous as an actor—not to mention his reputation as 'the man who thrashed the Prince of Wales'—and this alone was enough to give the Theatre Royal appeal. Apart from that, his experience and his contacts enabled him to engage the finest theatrical talents available.

The most important achievement of Johnston's management was undoubtedly his booking of one of the greatest actors of all time, Edmund Kean. Local history, unfortunately, has not been kind to Kean. In Glasgow he is chiefly remembered for one disastrous performance in 1817, when he was plainly very drunk and acted in dumb show, the received mythology being that this was his only appearance in the city. This is very far from being the truth.

Apart from the fact that, even before Johnston booked him, Kean had acted in Glasgow on a number of occasions—as a strolling player, struggling to support his wife and family—he was to make regular appearances in the future. In the early 1820s, Kean made an attempt to settle on the island of Bute and would often act in the city during this time. As a matter of fact, Kean probably played Glasgow more often than any other city outside London.

Kean's 1815 Glasgow season was the very opposite of a disaster. He arrived fresh from his 1814 triumph at Drury Lane, where his performances had saved the theatre from bankruptcy and created a revolution in English acting. This sensation had been transmitted north by the press and, on Kean's arrival, the streets were thronged and the theatre was packed every night to witness the new star's interpretations of Shylock, Iago and Hamlet.

Johnston, who probably knew Kean first as a strolling player, must have been well pleased with this season, which seemed to promise a bright new future for the Glasgow stage. The fulfilment of such promise, however, was fated not to be of his concern. Just as things were going well in Glasgow, his Irish creditors caught up with him and, since he was unable to settle with them, he soon found himself in the Debtor's Jail in Dundee.

Just how long he was obliged to remain there is not known, but it could not have been more than a few months because, almost immediately, his fortunes took a turn which was very much for the better. Suddenly, unaccountably, Johnston's acting career was revived. In 1816, he was engaged to play the leading rôle of Sir Archy Macsarcasm in a revival of Macklin's *Love à la Mode* at Covent Garden.

What occasioned Johnston's rehabilitation is difficult to guess—it could have had nothing to do with his godfather, who had fallen from grace by this time— but the fact is that, from 1816 on, he was able to act once more on the London stage. He followed his success in *Love à la Mode* with another Macklin revival, playing Sir Pertinax Macsycophant in *Man of the World*. This was followed by a succession of rôles, including Pierre in *Venice Observ'd* and Baltimore in the first production of Joanna Baillie's *The Election*. Then, in 1818, Johnston made what must be considered the most serious artistic misjudgement of his career, when he accepted the rôle of Rob Roy Macgregor in George Soane's adaptation of the novel by Sir Walter Scott.

On all the available evidence, Rob Roy ought to have been the perfect rôle for Johnston. His looks, his physical presence, his Scottish background, his association in the public mind with tartan—even, indeed, his period of exile as an outlaw from the stage—all appear to indicate that he would have been the perfect choice for the embodiment of Scott's romantic hero. Yet, although Johnston was to play the part on a number of occasions, Rob was never to be a lucky rôle for him.

On this occasion, it was a complete disaster. The fact is the George Soane's *Rob Roy* is possibly the worst adaptation of any novel ever made; not so much a travesty as a complete emasculation. (Soane's plot—a grotesque and unconvincing love story, featuring Rob and Diana Vernon, with Helen Macgregor transformed into Rob's mother—owes more to the biblical tale of Samson and Delilah than anything Sir Walter Scott ever wrote.) To make matters worse, a successful version of the novel appeared at Covent Garden in the same year. This was Isaac Pocock's *Rob Roy*, written for the rising new star of William Charles Macready, and destined to become the most popular play that the Scottish theatre has ever known.

Although Johnston later played Pocock's Rob several times in Scotland, his performance in Soane's version rather ruined his chances in London. When Pocock's *Rob Roy* was revived at Drury Lane in 1821, Johnston appeared in the subsidiary rôle of Dougal. This seems to suggest that his career was on the wane, but he was to play one more leading rôle in London. This was later in 1821, at the Olympic Theatre in an adaptation from the French, entitled *The Solitary*. Johnston was commended by *The Drama* for his performance in this rôle, but the production—and Johnston's London career—ended in somewhat unfortunate circumstances. The *Drury Lane Journal* for 9 September, 1822, carries the following entry: 'Johnston, Tayleure and Oxberry came delegated from the Olympic Theatre to say that they had struck, their salaries not being paid from six to eight weeks'.

In 1823, Johnston returned to Edinburgh to embark on a brand new venture. In 1803, the Pantheon Theatre—as the Edinburgh Equestrian Circus was now called—had been taken over by a musician, Natali Corri. It then became Corri's New Room, a concert hall and assembly room, devoted to dancing and card-playing. Nine years later, Corri decided to extend his activities by applying to the Lord Chamberlain for a license to produce plays. Although this application was unsuccessful, Corri managed to produce plays by astutely utilising a curious loop-hole in the law. Apparently, the Patent held by the Theatre Royal gave that theatre an exclusive right to perform plays *which had been licensed by the Lord Chamberlain*. By restricting his programme to plays which had *not* received such a license, Corri was able to carry on production in the building, which he re-named the Pantheon in 1812, for the best part of the next decade. In 1818, however, Corri—who used to say that he was so unlucky that were he 'to turn baker, people would give up eating bread'—went bankrupt and the Pantheon was put up for sale. Corri remained as manager until his death five years later.

Johnston had been interested in the Pantheon for some time. In 1813, he had sought to escape from his Irish troubles by attempting to take over the management and had made an application to the Lord Chamberlain in order to do so. This application had, of course, been unsuccessful and Corri remained in charge. In 1823, however, Corri died and Johnston was given his chance. His first act was to re-name the theatre yet again—it was now the Caledonian.

> After having undergone considerable alterations, this Theatre (late Pantheon) opened on Saturday evening last, under the direction of Mr H. Johnston. The stage has been brought forward about twelve feet; and what was formerly the ring is now converted into the pit. The general effect of the house presents a warm and comfortable appearance. The private boxes on the stage are hung with the Rob Roy tartan, as is also the drapery of the drop-scene, representing a camp on the Braid Hills, with a view of Edinburgh in the distance. Previous to the commencement of the performances, Mr H. Johnston came forward and was hailed with enthusiastic cheers of approbation.

The above notice appeared in the *Edinburgh Observer* of January, 1823, just a week after the opening of Johnston's first—and, as it turned out, only—season at the Caledonian.

To anyone familiar with the ongoing campaign for a Scottish National Theatre, that season will have a curiously familiar look. Apart from the comedy, *Tom and Jerry*, and the pantomime, *Mother Goose*, there is a strong Scottish dimension in the programme. The season opened with William Barrymore's *Gilderoy*, based on the true story of the Highland outlaw Patrick Macgregor—possibly the model for Scott's fictional Rob Roy—who was hanged in 1638. This was followed by a stage version of Scott's *Peveril of the Peak* (which had only just been published) and the first production ever of *The Jolly Beggars* by Robert Burns. Added to this, Johnston had gathered together a company of Scottish actors from all over the provinces: it is difficult to escape the impression that some kind of initiative had been planned.

If this was indeed the case, it was an initiative that ended in failure, not only for the company but for Johnston himself. He resigned his lease on the theatre after three months, probably because the lack of business made it impossible for him to continue. Apart from the fact that he simply did not have the money to make a long term investment in the Caledonian, the financial struggles of the past had probably taken their toll on his credit rating.

After the failure of the Caledonian, Johnston entered the twilight of his career and we are only given brief glimpses of him from then on. The management of the Caledonian was taken over by Corbet Ryder of Perth, who immediately engaged Johnston to play a short season of three nights. Ironically enough, the rôle he chose for that occasion was that of Pocock's *Rob Roy*.

Johnston then disappeared into the provinces, finding engagements wherever he could, in locations as far apart as Plymouth and Perth. Seven years later, he returned to the Caledonian, now under the management of Charles Bass, for a season of four nights. No details of these performances survive, but they must have been given with mixed feelings; this was the theatre where he had thrown flowers at Nanette's feet and where he had seen his hopes of a successful management finally come to an end. Whatever his feelings, however, this was to be his last appearance in the city of his youth.

In 1837, Johnston decided to try his luck in America and appeared for a season at the National Theatre in Church Street, New York. This venture, however, did not repair his fortunes and, indeed, ended rather unpleasantly. After his New York season, he applied for an engagement at the Chestnut Street Theatre, Philadelphia, then under the management of Francis Courtney Wemyss. Wemyss, who came from Glasgow, had good reason to remember Johnston. In 1815, during Johnston's Glasgow management, Wemyss had been trying to make a start in the theatre. Johnston had given him what ought to have been his first job, except that, on learning that the young actor's family were opposed to a stage career, he had withdrawn the offer. Now that the boot, as it were, was on the other foot, Wemyss lost no time in rejecting Johnston's application. In his autobiography, published a decade later, he tells us that Johnston was 'refused for want of talent, having become perfectly superannuated'. Whether this is an indication of Johnston's failing powers or Wemyss's meanness of spirit is impossible to say. In any event, Johnston, feeling that America had nothing to offer him, packed his bags and returned to England.

His last days were spent in obscurity. According to one source—the Irish actor, Walter Donaldson, in his *Recollections of an Actor* (London, 1865)—Johnston's career ended in Cumberland, where he ran a circuit of small theatres. On the other hand, Walter Baynham in his *History of the Glasgow Stage*, tells us that these days were spent in London, where Johnston 'lived off the charity of his brother actors'. Although Baynham is inaccurate in other details, this is probably true. Johnston was always popular with his colleagues. He died in 1845, at the age of 67, and is buried in Lambeth, the borough that provided him with refuge after his contretemps with the Prince of Wales.

Henry Erskine Johnston was the first Scottish actor of note, the first to enjoy any kind of reputation and following. A critic who was his contemporary, Gilliland, describes him as a 'useful' actor, using the word in that curious English sense, suggesting quality that is not quite of the first rank. At his best, he may not have been in the same league as Kean and Mrs Siddons, but he was certainly very good indeed. The following assessment of his acting appeared in the *Monthly Mirror* in October, 1797, just after his London debut.

> His voice is unusually flexible, and its tones various; soft, sweet, melting, strong, piercing, full, capable of any depression or any elevation...His countenance is expressive, his figure is pretty but boyish; it wants height and substance for an universal character, though it sits well with the youth of Norval. His action is animated and often graceful; the same may be said for his deportment. His pathos is indeed inimitable; it flows from the pure source of feeling and cannot fail.

Johnston's career would establish a pattern for other Scottish actors to follow;

initial success in Scotland, followed by a move south. It is a pattern which continues to this day and, from the point of view of the professional actor, there is nothing in the least reprehensible about it. Yet it does mean that the Scottish Theatre has been obliged, throughout its history, to endure a perpetual haemorrhage of its finest talent. There is a certain irony in the fact that the initiative that effectively ended Johnston's career—his ill-fated management of the Edinburgh Caledonian—may have been made in an attempt to reverse this trend.

If this was indeed the case, there is a further irony, having to do with what must have been the main reason for Johnston's failure at the Caledonian. Another actor, in another theatre, not a stone's throw away in the same city, was creating a similar initiative; a successful one, with which Johnston, for all his talent, could not compete. It is to this actor—William Murray of the Theatre Royal, Edinburgh—that we must now turn our attention.

Chapter Three

SURPASSED BY NONE—
WILLIAM MURRAY

Let our exertions be made, then let them be judged. It is true that this concern labours under many difficulties; but what hope have we of surmounting these difficulties, but by endeavouring in every way to meet the wishes of the public?

These words were spoken on 20 May, 1815, on the stage of the Theatre Royal, Edinburgh, by the man who, over the next 36 years, would not only dominate and transform completely the Edinburgh stage, but would set the agenda of the Scottish Theatre for the next century. His name was William Henry Murray and he was a complete man of the theatre: an actor, a playwright, a brilliant stage-manager and, by no means least, a theatre manager of genius.

In order to fully understand the magnitude of Murray's achievement, we must return to the situation that obtained in the Edinburgh theatre after the passing of the Theatres Act of 1737. As mentioned at the end of Chapter 1, activity was restricted to unlicensed performances and these continued, at the Taylor's Hall, for some five years under the management of Thomas Este. In 1745, however, the foundation stone of a new theatre in the Canongate was laid and by the following year the house was completed.

The origins of this building are shrouded in mystery; one presumes that it was built on the site originally leased for the purpose almost 20 years earlier by the Edinburgh Company of Players, but the identity of the original owner is completely unknown. For the next five years, it was known as the Canongate Concert Hall, competing with the Taylor's Hall as a venue for unlicensed performances. Then, in 1751, the name was changed to that of the Canongate Theatre and it became the focus of an initiative to bring a legal theatre to Edinburgh.

This initiative came in 1751 from a group of landowners and senior legal figures, led by Lord Patrick Elibank and the Hon. Andrew Pringle of Alemoor. The motives of these people were pretty much at one with those expressed by Lord Glenorchy in his withdrawal speech to the House of Commons (see Chapter 2), but they had been given an additional impetus by the defeat of the Jacobite army at Culloden five years earlier. This seemed to usher in a period of political stability such as Scotland had not known for several centuries. There was a great desire on the part of the Edinburgh upper class to bring their society into line with that of the new age and, to this end, a theatre of the best quality was deemed essential. After discussing the matter—and taking, no doubt the best advice—the Elibank group made an approach to John Lee, the leading actor at Drury Lane.

Lee was an actor whose overweening vanity tended to detract from his considerable ability. 'He was forever doing the honours of his face', wrote his contemporary, the playwright-manager, Samuel Foote, 'he affected uncommon long pauses and frequently took such out-of-the-way pains with emphasis and articulation that the natural actor seldom appeared.'

For all of that, Lee was very much in demand at the time. Besides playing leading rôles at Drury Lane, he had also been appearing at Covent Garden—a situation which had recently involved him in an acrimonious dispute with his manager, the great David Garrick—and he was clearly in the market for an opportunity which would enable him to build on his success. The proposition he received from the Elibank group seemed most attractive. If Lee would agree to come to Edinburgh and establish a theatre company, arrangements would be made enabling him to purchase the theatre for the sum of £645, payable in four instalments, spread over three years. In addition to this, an annuity of £100 a year for the next five years would be secured for Lee, provided that he remained in Edinburgh for this period. On the surface, this seemed an exciting opportunity and Lee lost no time in accepting.

As matters turned out, Lee's management was a complete and utter disaster. The plain fact of the matter is that it was completely impossible for Lee—or anyone else—to create the kind of theatre company that the Elibank group wanted. The tiny audience meant too few performances. The Edinburgh season lasted only a few months—and, even then, involved no more than two, perhaps three, performances per week—whereas Lee was required to engage his actors on an annual basis. It was as if one of our modern theatres was required to carry out business for the year solely on its earnings from the Edinburgh Festival.

After little more than 12 months, Lee was forced to sign over his ownership of the theatre to the Elibank group—who would, however, accept no responsibility for his considerable debts—and, after two years service as manager, he was despatched from Edinburgh in the most shameful manner. One night, Lee came off the stage—after performing, appropriately enough, the rôle of King Lear—to find that he was under arrest, all his goods had been impounded and his wife and children turned out into the street!

Although none of Lee's successors suffered a similar fate, neither did any of them prosper in their management. The only one to have any kind of real success was West Digges, who was responsible for the premiere production of Home's *Douglas*, described in Chapter 2. Digges made something of an impression by virtue of his own good looks and the notoriety which surrounded his romantic association with two actresses: the popular Sarah Ward and the dangerously beautiful George Anne Bellamy. His mistreatment of the first and his besotted devotion to the other has earned Digges a footnote in the history of the English stage, but no amount of scandal could possibly make the Canongate Theatre pay. As a matter of fact, the most noteworthy events that took place in this sadly troubled playhouse were not performances but riots.

In 1760, there was the Footmen's Riot, when some Highland footmen—who carried their employers to the theatre in sedan chairs and were admitted free— were evicted by the City Guard for barracking a performance of a play by James Townley called *High Life Below Stairs*, which they considered to be insulting to the servant class. This, however, was little more than a scuffle and a much more serious affray took place in January, 1767, when the audience ran amok and all but destroyed the theatre. The cause of this riot was a popular Irish actor called George Stayley, who had recently staged a very successful production of Ramsay's *The Gentle Shepherd*. In spite of this success, the management—then in the hands of a rather anonymous individual from Newcastle called David Beat, who seems to have been a merchant rather than an actor—refused Stayley employment, making his many supporters so angry that they simply smashed the place to pieces.

The Stayley Riot really spelled the end for the Canongate Theatre. Although it was to have one other manager—the talented but indolent David Ross—this was only a temporary tenancy. Ross had secured a Royal Patent and simply made use of the Canongate while the Theatre Royal was being built. Thus it came to pass that the first legal performance of a play in Scotland—a translation from the French of Thomas Corneille, entitled *The Earl of Essex*—took place on 19 December, 1767, in the Canongate Theatre. Two years later, in November 1769, the Theatre Royal opened its doors for the first time and the Canongate Theatre disappeared forever. Its ending is shrouded in as much mystery as its beginning, so much so that one is unable to pinpoint exactly when the building was pulled down. All that remains of it in Edinburgh today is the name of the close where it was situated: Playhouse Close.

The new Theatre Royal opened in a blaze of glory, with a performance of Sir Richard Steele's *The Conscious Lovers*, preceded by a prologue from the pen of James Boswell. With this opening, theatre in Scotland seemed to have been given a fresh start. So many of the difficulties of the past had apparently disappeared; the population was growing, political tensions were fading from memory, the Union was a fact of life and 'the English language' was on everyone's lips. Most important of all, the new theatre was completely legal, part of the exciting project of the New Town.

Unfortunately, although this novelty produced a rush of business in the first few weeks, the effect soon wore off. Three years later, in 1770, Ross had become disillusioned with management and made over the theatre on lease to Samuel Foote, then manager of the Haymarket in London. The Haymarket only had a licence to perform in the summer months, so Foote conceived the audacious—

for that time—experiment of transferring his entire company to Edinburgh for the winter. Although Foote was rumoured to have made a considerable profit during that season, this experiment was not repeated. Foote, in his turn, signed over the lease to West Digges, who made a brief (and unsuccessful) return to Edinburgh. After that, it was all downhill. Ross retained ownership of the theatre, but did not appear to take much interest in it. It is, in fact, a measure of Ross's fecklessness that, when John Jackson bought the theatre in 1781, just 12 years after it had come into existence, he had practically to rebuild the place. As Jackson tells us in his *History of the Scottish Stage*:

> I cannot devise any thing so wretched. There were neither scenes, wardrobe, or any other appendage suitable to a Theatre Royal. There was not even a roof; the thing so called was like a sieve, which let the rain through in a million of places. With the house in this deranged state, I commenced manager.

John Jackson, who was an entrepreneur rather than an artist—and whose career will be discussed more fully in a later chapter—was altogether the most formidable theatre manager that Scotland had seen until then; shrewd and resourceful, full of fighting spirit and a gritty determination to see his plans through. Although he maintained his own company, the main strategy of his management—not only in Edinburgh, but in the many theatres he owned throughout Scotland—was to induce the most popular actors of the London theatre to come north. The tragic genius of James Henderson, the notorious beauty of Dorothy Jordan, the prodigious precocity of Master Betty, the pert vivacity of Jane Pope and the comic talents of such as Tom King, Lee Lewes and Jack Bannister were all seen under Jackson's management. Without a doubt, however, the most impressive achievement of Jackson's career was his engagement of the greatest actress of the age, Sarah Siddons.

Mrs Siddons was then at the very height of her powers, enjoying a popularity that cut across all classes and divisions of society, from the highest to the lowest. As Yvonne Ffrench puts it:

> In Edinburgh Mrs Siddons can have had little cause to doubt her power of charming when she could earn tributes from the working classes in language that was worthy of Burns. 'Ah, weill do I ken that sweet voice, that garr'd me greet sae sair yestreen' was the passing compliment of a servant out marketing who recognized the deep, melodious tones.

The seasons played by the great actress from 1783 on demonstrated just how far it was possible for the theatre to go in Scotland; they drew huge audiences from every part of the population, creating so much excitement that they have since won a place in urban Scottish folklore. They also made a great deal of money for Jackson and the Theatre Royal.

Even Jackson, however, could not withstand the interfering prejudices of the lairds and lawyers who sought to impose their will on theatrical affairs. Nothing exemplifies this more than a rather shameful episode which took place in 1788, involving a tall, handsome, imposing and popular actor called James Fennell. Fennell—who would later achieve a measure of distinction on the early American stage—had been hired by Jackson for the specific purpose of giving support to Mrs Siddons, who was playing her second season in Edinburgh.

Coming from a prosperous background and having received his education at Eton and Cambridge, Fennell did not consider that his employment as an actor was any reason to lower his social ambitions. In Edinburgh, he made an attempt to enter polite society and this, according to John Genest in his *Account of the English Stage*, 'gave offence to several gentlemen'.

One evening, as the company were about to take the stage in a performance of Otway's *Venice Observ'd*, Jackson received an anonymous note informing him that, if Fennell was allowed to appear, the show would be stopped. Knowing the Edinburgh propensity for riot, Jackson must have been concerned but, to his great credit, he ignored the threat. A section of the audience began to boo and hiss as soon as Fennell appeared and, when this continued on the following night, the actor took steps to identify his detractors, as a result of which he raised an action against one of them for conspiring to drive him from his employment. Jackson then received another letter—and this was certainly not anonymous.

Sir,
We are of the opinion that Mr Fennell's late deportment to the public, and your conduct as manager with regard to that matter, require a very ample apology from both, testifying your deep regret for having failed in the respect due to them; and if Mr Fennell fails to make such an apology, you ought immediately to dismiss him. And we take this method of intimating to you that, if this opinion is not complied with...neither we nor our families will henceforth frequent your theatre, or shew you any countenance as manager, except that, from our high regard for Mrs Siddons, we shall postpone executing our resolution till her engagement expires.

The letter was signed by Robert Dundas, Solicitor-General of Scotland, and 164 gentlemen of the legal profession.

An actor, it would seem, could be treated as a celebrity, but was not to be considered a suitable member of society. These people could see no inconsistency in persecuting Fennell while simultaneously honouring his leading lady. At the conclusion of that season, Mrs Siddons was presented with a piece of gold plate weighing 144 ounces by those very same 'gentlemen' who wanted to force her colleague out of his employment. As for Fennell, Jackson had no choice: he had to let the actor go.

The acceptance of such double standards practised by its leading patrons hardly made for the kind of ambience in which the theatre could develop artistically, culturally or, indeed, commercially. Three years later, Jackson himself was gone, declared bankrupt in spite of all his energetic inventiveness. To be absolutely fair, however, Jackson may have been misled in this respect, in much the same way as Lee had been 40 years earlier. Writing of his Edinburgh experience in his memoirs, he hints of promised financial backing which was not forthcoming.

> This necessary and laudable endeavour led me into great and numerous expenses; which, however, were not run into hastily, but upon very mature deliberation and under the strongest assurance of a pecuniary support to no inconsiderable amount. In that I was disappointed and from that disappointment the deficiency in my finances arose.

The Theatre Royal passed into the hands of Mrs Siddons' brother, Stephen Kemble. Despite frequent appearances by his sister—who appeared in Edinburgh whenever Stephen's treasury was in need of funds—Kemble enjoyed no more success than any of his predecessors in the Edinburgh theatre had done and, in fact, became extremely unpopular. When he tried to make a Farewell Address on the occasion of his departure in 1800, he was booed off the stage.

For the next nine years, the Theatre Royal staggered along under a succession of managers, gradually becoming more and more tatty and disreputable. Prostitutes thronged the foyer, the pit was thick with pickpockets, and muggers—or footpads, as they were then known—lurked in its environs. Disreputable or not, however, it was as legal as Drury Lane and Covent Garden and this was a matter of pride to the wealthy élite who were its sponsors.

Quite clearly, some kind of radical measure had to be taken. In 1809, a new group of trustees purchased shares in the theatre. Among them was a 38-year-old lawyer who was gaining a reputation as a poet and who was, even then, secretly writing fiction; at the time he was plain Mr Walter Scott. It was through Scott's efforts that the Patent was secured for Henry Siddons, son of the great Sarah.

Siddons was a man of energy and intelligence, a manager who was more in the Jackson mould than that of his uncle. It is true that, like Stephen, he continued to rely on appearances by his mother, but he engaged other leading actors from London, too—including his more famous uncle, John Philip Kemble, and the great comedian, Charles Mathews. At the same time, he began to build up a talented Edinburgh company, which included his wife, the former Miss Harriet Murray, and her brother, William. When Siddons unexpectedly died in 1814, these two inherited control of the theatre. Harriet's main contribution was as an actress—'Edinburgh's own Mrs Siddons'—although, as we shall see, she took her responsibilities as Patent holder very seriously indeed. For the most part, however, she was content to leave the day-to-day running of the theatre to her brother.

William Murray's background is both interesting and, to some extent, revealing of his character and the chosen direction of his career. Although he was born into a theatrical family, the theatricality was of very recent provenance. His grandfather was Sir John Murray of Broughton, a leading Jacobite and one-time secretary to Prince Charles Edward Stuart. When King James VIII was proclaimed at the cross of Edinburgh in 1745, Sir John's wife, the beautiful Lady Margaret, appeared at the ceremony on horseback, decorated with ribbons and

William Henry Murray by R Alexander

holding a drawn sword in her hand. Unfortunately—somewhat ironically—Sir John was to find that, while he was to be unfaithful to his Prince, Lady Margaret was to be no less unfaithful to *him*.

In the July of 1747, Sir John Murray surrendered to the Lord Justice Clerk in Edinburgh and was sent to London where he immediately set about saving his skin by turning King's Evidence against other Jacobites, thus earning the soubriquet of 'the most hated man in Scotland'. Shortly after that, on discovering Lady Margaret's infidelity, he divorced her, sold his estate and moved south, where he married Dorothy Webb, a Quakeress. Sir John had six children with his second wife, the eldest of whom was Charles Murray, William Murray's father. This was the first actor in the family.

As actors go, Charles Murray appears to have been competent rather than successful. John Genest, in his *Account of the English Stage*, describes him as 'interesting rather than great, and suited for secondary parts rather than primary...especially commended for the dignity of his old men'. Apart from William, Charles Murray had two other children who were to make their mark upon the stage: Harriet, of course, and Maria, who married an actor called Joe Cowell and gave birth to one of the first great stars of the Victorian Music Hall, Sam Cowell.

William Henry Murray was born in Bath in 1790 and made his first appearance on any stage at the age of four when, for his father's benefit, he appeared as Puck in *A Midsummer Night's Dream*. When Charles Murray moved to London two years later, young William naturally accompanied him and he grew up in Covent Garden, learning his trade and occasionally playing small parts. It was at Covent Garden, too, that he was to encounter the most important influence on his life, Charles Farley.

Farley was one of the most exciting and versatile performers that ever graced a stage; an actor, a singer, a dancer and a stage-manager of genius, best known for the spectacular effects he produced in pantomime, which was his acknowledged speciality. He was also a fine teacher, always ready to pass on his skills to anyone who was interested, his most famous pupil being the great clown, Joseph Grimaldi. In a career of over 40 years, he rarely performed outside Covent Garden, where he had a great influence on his younger colleagues. Farley taught Murray everything he knew about production, a debt that Murray was to acknowledge in one of the last of his public speeches, delivered more than 50 years later.

When Murray first arrived in Edinburgh, he was just 19 years old and full of enthusiasm. At first, he did not work at the Theatre Royal but at Natali Corri's theatre in Leith Walk—formerly the Edinburgh Equestrian Circus, later to become the Pantheon, the Caledonian etc.—to which Siddons had transferred the Patent. In addition to acting there, Murray appears to have taken charge of production but, according to his own account, he met with little success and two years later, in 1811, he moved with the rest of the company to the Theatre Royal. For the next four years, the theatre continued to struggle and Murray might well have returned to London—he had a number of offers to do so throughout his career—had it not been for the untimely death of Henry Siddons in 1815.

It was at this time that Murray made the speech that was quoted at the beginning of this chapter. Even as he spoke, he knew the theatre to be in debt to the tune of £21,000—an enormous sum of money in 1815. He also knew of the difficulties with which his predecessors had been afflicted and the consequences for himself and the theatre should he fail. He decided, quite simply, that he would not fail. At 25 years of age, he had a radical, adventurous spirit which often delighted in living dangerously, and a clear theatrical vision which was, in many respects, decades in advance of his time.

From the beginning, Murray set out to popularise theatre in Scotland; theatre as an art and theatre as a pastime. He began by cleaning up the Theatre Royal, improving the decor and generally making the place more appealing. He evicted the prostitutes from the foyer—although he never succeeded in getting rid of them altogether and they continued to haunt the approaches to the theatre for as long as it was in existence—and installed gas lighting, which was a great innovation at the time. It may also have been at this point—although it is difficult to be sure—that the number of playing nights during the season was increased to a full week.

Murray made every attempt to gain as complete a knowledge as possible of what his audience wanted and would begin and end each season with one of his famous 'addresses', in which he discussed his plans directly with his patrons. A selection of these speeches was published at the time of his retirement in 1851 and, their ephemeral nature notwithstanding, they still make entertaining reading.

On the stage, Murray instituted production values which were far higher than any that had been previously known. Besides introducing an innovative authenticity to setting and costume, he brought a greater discipline to rehearsal. At that time, actors were accustomed to studying alone and rehearsals were rather desultory affairs, involving little more than a series of informal readings of the play, with perhaps some discussion regarding movement. Murray was one of the first managers anywhere to insist that the cast conduct themselves at rehearsals in exactly the same manner as they would in performance. As far as programmming was concerned, he followed the practice, instituted by John Jackson, of engaging star names—Edmund Kean, Sarah Siddons, Charles Mathews, William Charles Macready, Helen Faucit and most of the leading lights of the London stage appeared at the Theatre Royal under Murray's management—but he placed much greater emphasis on the use of Scottish talent.

This, in fact, was the key to Murray's success. With the possible exception of Henry Siddons, he was the first Edinburgh manager since Allan Ramsay to acknowledge the importance of giving his work a Scottish dimension. To William Murray, the theatre was not a place of instruction where the Edinburgh bourgeoisie could learn to imitate London manners, but a place of entertainment and stimulation which was central to the life of the whole community. While he certainly never neglected the great traditions of English drama, he understood immediately—as all too few have done, before or since—that, unless Scottish aspirations are addressed and answered, the theatre had no future in Scotland.

He had begun to pursue this policy very early on, before the death of Siddons, in fact. During his time at the Leith Walk house, Murray was involved in the production of a number of Scottish plays: Joanna Baillie's *Family Legend*, two pieces by unknown authors, *Caledonia* and *The Heiress of Strathearn* and, significantly enough, in view of what was to follow, an adaptation of Scott's poem, *The Lady of the Lake*, by the actor Daniel Terry. When Murray took over the management of the Theatre Royal, he immediately acquired the rights of Terry's adaptation of the latest novel to come from the pen of the Author of Waverley for production in the following season.

This was *Guy Mannering*, the first of the so-called 'Waverley Dramas' to be seen on the Edinburgh stage. Although this first production was not a success, Murray had enough belief in the play to revive it in the following season with a change of cast. The part of Dominie Sampson had been unsuccessfully played by an English comedian called Russell and Murray decided to replace him with a Scottish actor from Glasgow called Charles Mackay. Business increased immediately, with the result that Murray and Mackay formed a professional relationship which would last for the rest of their working lives.

Two years later, on 15 February 1819, when Mackay took the stage in the part of Bailie Nicol Jarvie in Murray's first production of *Rob Roy*, it was the beginning of a bright new era in the history of the Scottish Stage. When the still anonymous author of *Rob Roy* (Scott had not revealed himself as a novelist at this time and would not do so for another eight years) saw the production, he dashed off the following note to his adaptor.

> Murray has netted upwards of £3000 on Rob Roy; to be sure the man who played the Bailie made a piece of acting equal to whatever has been seen in the profession. For my own part, I was actually electrified by the truth, spirit and humour which he put into the part. It was the living Nicol Jarvie; conceited, pragmatical, cautious, generous, proud of his connection with Rob Roy, frightened for him at the same time, and yet extremely desirous to interfere with him as an adviser. The tone in which he seemed to give him up for a lost man after having provoked him into some burst of Highland violence, 'Ah, Rab, Rab!' was quite inimitable. I do assure you I never saw a thing better played.

Rob Roy provided a breakthrough which would, in time, solve all the problems of the Theatre Royal. Over the next 32 years, Murray would mount more than 20 adaptations of Waverley novels on the stage of the Theatre Royal: as well as *Rob Roy*, there was *The Heart of Midlothian*, *The Bride of Lammermoor*, *The Legend of Montrose*, *The Fair Maid of Perth*, *The Fortunes of Nigel*, *The Antiquary*, *St Ronan's Well* and many others. Not all of them scored huge box-office success—some of them, indeed, were outright failures—but that is scarcely the point. The Waverley dramas had an appeal that cut across class differences, reaching every section of the population. In this way Murray succeeded, ironically, in achieving what the Elibank group had failed to do a century earlier. During Murray's management, Edinburgh became possessed of a theatre whose status was every bit as high as that of Covent Garden or Drury Lane—and this was recognised by everyone in the theatre world.

There was another, more important, consequence of this success. Indigenous theatrical development—which, as we have seen, was stifled by the withdrawal of the Glenorchy Bill in 1740—was at last taking place. The Waverley Dramas, together with a dozen or so plays by other Scottish authors, ultimately laid the foundations of a new theatrical tradition, identified by its distinctively Scottish style.

This style, which came to be known by the term 'National Drama', bears a marked resemblance to the popular style of Melodrama—which was then, of course, in its heyday—but there are at least three important differences. National Drama is specifically Scottish, not only in setting and language, but in terms of its cultural perception; its characters are altogether less artificial and more down-to-earth; it makes much more use of music and song. In short, whereas Melodrama usually draws a moral, National Drama is content simply to tell a story. It is a style which enjoyed a mass audience for more than a century and its influence, in one form or another, can be detected in the Scottish Theatre even today. Although its creation would not have been possible without the imagination of Scott and the comic genius of Charles Mackay, a major contribution was made by the many talents of William Murray.

As an actor, Murray's talent was big enough to prompt the belief that he must have done himself less than justice. Fanny Kemble, one of the great stars of the nineteenth century and Murray's cousin through marriage, once described him as 'the finest actor I have ever seen on any stage'—but Murray did not conduct his acting career as if this were the case. Unlike most leading actors of his time, he did not confine himself to a few leading rôles, repeated over and over, with only the occasional departure into a new play. As a matter of fact, Murray did not even confine himself to leading rôles, as a brief glance at his record immediately reveals: Captain Thornton in *Rob Roy*, Jonathan Oldbuck in *The Antiquary*, Craigengelt in *The Bride of Lammermoor*, George Heriot in *The Fortunes of Nigel*, Peregrine Touchwood in *St Ronan's Well*, Figaro in *The Barber of Seville*, Newman Noggs in *Nicholas Nickleby*, Bumble in *Oliver Twist*, Falstaff, Caliban, Sir Anthony Absolute and Roland Graeme in his own *Mary Stuart*. Although this indicates a quite astonishing range, it seems likely that this was brought about by necessity rather than inclination. Acting, although an important department of his work, was never the centre of his interest.

Although it might seem anachronistic to describe Murray as a director—the term was not coined until the twentieth century—this is justified by the belief that Murray was considerably ahead of his time. In many ways, he had both the temperament and sense of vision of a Stanislavsky or a Peter Brook. He was extremely innovative and a list of his productions would prove just as wide ranging as that of his rôles, covering every form of drama, from Shakespeare and Sheridan to farce and pantomime. Even in his development of National Drama, he was continually experimenting. He never seemed to be satisfied with the existing versions of some of the plays and was perpetually ringing the changes, on one occasion compiling a script of *The Heart of Midlothian* from what he considered to be the best scenes of all previous versions. Unfortunately, he had some of the less admirable inclinations of the modern director, too—particularly when it came to his dealings with living playwrights. He paid them as little as possible and, whenever he could get away with it, nothing at all. As a matter of fact, it was Murray's acquisition by theft of a manuscript—J R Planché's *Charles XII*—that led to the first piece of legislation to protect the work of playwrights: the Dramatic Authors Act of 1833.

The fact that Murray was a man who had a reputation for fair dealing is at odds with his shabby, somewhat cavalier treatment of playwrights—and this becomes even more inexplicable when one considers that Murray was a fairly accomplished playwright himself. He was a playwright in the old, nineteenth century sense of the word; a playmaker, a theatrical functionary whose main job was to prepare scripts for a particular audience in a particular place. Since he did not always claim credit for his work as author, we are unable to gain a clear perspective on his output, particularly where adaptations are concerned—although we do know that he was responsible for a stage version of *Oliver Twist* and a

An Estimate of the Average Receipts, and Expenditure, in the Theatre-Royal, supposing 35 Weeks to constitute a Season.

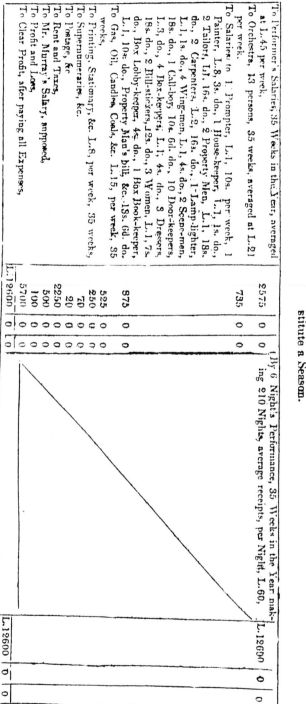

				By 6 Night's Performance, 35 Weeks in the Year, making 210 Nights, average receipts, per Night, L.60,	L.12600	0	0
To Performer's Salaries, 35 Weeks in the Year, averaged at L.45 per week,	2575	0	0				
To Orchestra, 13 persons, 35 weeks, averaged at L.21 per week;	735	0	0				
To Salaries, to 1 Prompter, L.1, 10s. per week, 1 Painter, L.8, 3s. do., 1 House-keeper, L.1, 1s. do., 2 Tailors, L1. 16s. do., 2 Property Men, L.1, 18s. do., 2 Carpenters, L.2, 16s. do., 1 Lamp-lighter, L.1, 1s. do., 4 Wing-men, L.1, 4s. do., 2 Scene-men, 18s. do., 1 Call-boy 10s. 6d. do., 10 Door-keepers, 1.3, do., 4 Box-keepers, L.1, 4s. do., 3 Women, 1.3, do., 2 Bill-stickers, 12s. do., 3 Women, L.1, 18s. do., 1 Box Book-keeper, L.1, 7s. do., Box Lobby-keeper, 4s. do., 1 Property Man's bill &c. 13s. 6d. do., L.1, 10s. do.,	975	0	0				
To Gas, Oil, Candles, Coals, &c. L.15, per week, 35 weeks,	525	0	0				
To Printing, Stationary, &c. L.8, per week, 35 weeks,	250	0	0				
To Supernumeraries, &c.	70	0	0				
To Postage, &c	20	0	0				
To Rent and Taxes,	2250	0	0				
To Mr. Murray's Salary, supposed,	500	0	0				
To Profit and Loss,	100	0	0				
To Clear Profit, after paying all Expenses,	5700	0	0				
	L.12600	0	0		L.12600	0	0

burlesque version of *Romeo and Juliet*. As far as his original drama is concerned—and here we have a much clearer notion of his authorship—his work is refreshingly free of literary pretension, his concerns being restricted completely to his own time and place. Yet his plays remain viable and could be presented, with little adjustment, even today. His most substantial piece—and certainly his most successful, enjoying countless revivals by many companies throughout the nineteenth century—is the three-act *Mary Stuart*, in which he displays a quite masterly command of Scottish history and language.

As actor, director, playwright and manager, Murray created a centre of excellence for other Scottish theatres to emulate—although, it must be said, *not* in Edinburgh. Once he became Patent holder in 1829 he was very jealous of his status and would challenge any interloper through the courts. If this seems dictatorial, it should be remembered that Murray was the first—and only—Edinburgh theatre manager to feel the necessity of such action. Neither Lee nor Digges, Ross, Jackson or Kemble ever felt the pressure of competition, which took place as a direct result of the audience that Murray had created. It was no more than natural that he should be jealous of his advantage.

The most noticeable effect of this new, expanded audience was to change the whole cultural environment. Since theatre was now genuinely popular, it was inevitably discussed with great animation, not only in terms of common intercourse, but in print, too. During the period of Murray's reign, no fewer than 17 theatre journals appeared regularly, creating a body of theatre criticism which was infinitely more lively than anything that had been seen previously. The following is an extract from one of those, the *Dramatic Censor* of 1830, and comes from the pen of its anonymous editor, who wrote under the pseudonym of 'Proteus Porcupine'. Edmund Kean had recently played a season of six nights at the Theatre Royal, supported—as was then the custom—by the resident company. In *Othello*, the part of Iago was taken by an actor called Barton, of whose performance a typically forthright assessment is made.

> Barton's Iago was one of the most decided failures we have seen lately on our stage. It was completely a misconception and presented no points of character. He made the villain a brave, honour-loving fellow—yet hard and acid as vinegar—peculiarities which were never designed to accompany the Iago of Shakespeare. His action was also most absurdly redundant: he used his arms like two immense levers and appeared inclined to knock everyone down with whom he came in conversation. Is it a natural defect, or an acquired habit which makes him speak in such a tremulous style? His voice, on Saturday evening, taken together with his bad acting and worst action, rendered the *tout ensemble* anything but agreeable. In short, his performance was ludicrous.

Under Murray, the Theatre Royal became a place where things happened, where they were noticed and reported. Perhaps the most spectacular example of this was an event which took place in 1846. At the time, it would seem to have been of little significance and was barely noticed—yet it was to have serious repercussions on the other side of the Atlantic.

In March 1846, the great tragedian William Charles Macready appeared at the Theatre Royal in a season which included a performance of *Hamlet*. A feature of Macready's Hamlet was a piece of business he carried out with a handkerchief in one of the early scenes. On this particular occasion, the great American actor, Edwin Forrest, who was touring Scotland at the time, was in the audience. When Forrest saw what Macready was doing with the handkerchief, for some unknown reason he took great offence, hissed loudly and walked out. It was a rather ill-mannered action on Forrest's part, but it did not interfere with the performance and nobody thought much about it at the time. A few days later, however, it was reported in London and created something of a furore. When Forrest opened there later that year, he was given a hostile reception by supporters of Macready. Forrest always blamed Macready for this and, three years later, when the English actor toured America, his American rival duplicated the tour, appearing in the same towns, at the same time, in the same plays as Macready was presenting. This led to a a somewhat hysterical factionalism—American actor v. English—which came to a head on 10 May, 1849 at the Astor Place Opera House in New York. During Macready's performance there, the greatest theatre riot in history took place, involving the New York Police, the State Militia and the Seventh Cavalry. Twenty-two people were killed and thirty-six wounded: Macready himself barely escaped with his life.

The small but significant part that the Theatre Royal played in the Astor Place Riot indicates that events that took place on the Edinburgh stage were likely to have repercussions elsewhere. Such an occurrence in any other theatre in Scotland would barely have been noticed. Murray himself enjoyed universal celebrity. This was so widespread that he adopted the habit of travelling incognito whenever he left Edinburgh. On one occasion, during a shooting holiday in the Highlands, he heard that there was a theatre in the locality and decided to pay it a visit. While dining at the local inn, he casually enquired of the waiter if they 'did things decently there'? He was surprised and delighted to be given the following reply: 'Deed they do, conseedrin the hoose is but smaa an the craturs pickit up onywhaur. Ye canna expect things to be preceesely as guid as in yer *ain* Theatre o Edinburgh, Mr Murray.'

In his private life, Murray was very much a family man. His first marriage, to the actress Ann Dyke, ended sadly with Ann's death in 1829, after which Murray married another actress, Ellen Gray. This second marriage produced two children, Henry and Harriet, both of whom had comfortable, if undistinguished, stage careers.

In his running of the theatre, Murray was a strict disciplinarian—both with his company and with himself—and became known as 'the Napoleon of managers'. He was small in stature, austere and not a little diffident in manner, yet possessed of a certain droll sense of humour. On 23 February, 1827, he was present at the famous occasion—a dinner in aid of the Edinburgh Theatrical Fund—when Sir Walter Scott revealed his authorship of the Waverley Novels. A few weeks later, Murray was approached for his opinion by two ladies who had been discussing the question of who had really written the plays of Shakespeare. One said it was Ben Jonson, the other that it was, indeed, the Bard of Avon. What did Mr Murray think? 'Neither of them' quipped Murray, 'It was Sir Walter Scott. He confessed it at a public meeting the other day!'

Despite this sense of humour, however, Murray was a man who persistently suffered from low spirits. Apparently, he lived in constant fear of bankruptcy and even after his retiral in 1851, he accepted acting engagements in Aberdeen and Dundee—in spite of the fact that it had been his poor health which had persuaded him to retire. Yet, according to his long-time assistant, the comedian H F Lloyd, he was so disillusioned with the theatrical profession that he gave away his private wardrobe and burned all his papers before leaving the Theatre Royal. He gave his last address to an Edinburgh audience on 22 October, 1851, before setting out for St Andrews, where he intended to settle. Less than seven months later, returning from a party on 5 May, 1852, William Murray collapsed and died.

Murray's influence cast a long shadow over Scottish Theatre history—as we shall see in the next few chapters. At this point, however, it seems appropriate to end this chapter as it began, with William Murray's own words, quoting from the last address he ever made to the audience of the Theatre Royal. On such occasions, it was—and still is—customary for a degree of humility to be displayed on the part of the departing actor. Murray maintained this convention well enough, except for one emotional moment, in which the pride he took in the Theatre Royal was quite evident.

> I make no claims to merit as an actor or a manager, but I own I *am* proud of the unvarying and inflexible integrity with which your support has enabled this establishment to meet its engagements under the most adverse and trying circumstances; an integrity equalled by few theatres—surpassed by none!

Chapter Four

A ROYAL COMPANY

The principal colours in the which the Theatre has been painted are pink and white. The boxes have been altered very much for the better and are now ornamented with diamonds formed of gold beading, in the centre of which very neat gold thistles, roses and shamrocks have been placed on a white ground. The Scots arms over the proscenium are now placed on a ground similar to the curtain, and this gives the whole proscenium a very warm appearance. The gas chandelier in the centre has undergone more material alterations than would strike the eye of a cursory observer. This, together with the re-painting, gives the roof a very unique appearance. The new drop-curtain is an architectural view of Edinburgh from the westward and is painted with considerable taste, as indeed the whole alterations display.

The above description of the interior of the Theatre Royal, Edinburgh appeared in the *Dramatic Review* in the November of 1822. In just over seven years, Murray had not only cleared the theatre's debts but had made enough money to enable his sister to purchase the theatre and to carry out further refurbishments. According to an estimate which had been made by the same journal—which Murray disputed in a fierce but rather unconvincing manner—the Theatre Royal was now earning an annual profit of just under £6,000.

For the first time in history, a Scottish theatre was prospering—and prospering, moreover, on its own terms. The success of the Theatre Royal owed absolutely nothing to the cultural ambitions of the Edinburgh élite, nor did it rely on the drawing power of the stars of the English theatre. The *Dramatic Review* was careful to point out that its calculation had specifically excluded the extra revenue generated by the visits of leading London actors. Occasional appearances by such as Edmund Kean and the glamorous Madame Vestris certainly generated a great deal of business, but it was *extra* business—the icing on the cake—and not at all essential to the theatre's success. As for the interfering influence of the lairds and lawyers which had created so many problems for such as Lee and Jackson, this was effectively silenced by the high reputation that the Theatre Royal enjoyed.

This reputation, of course, had not been created simply by the establishment of a finely furnished and well-appointed building. Indeed, it was not even a matter of the plays that were performed upon its stage, appealing as they were. The true source of William Murray's success lay in the company of actors he gathered around him, and it is with these actors that this chapter will be concerned.

The first point to be noted is that the Theatre Royal company never regarded itself as a provincial company and, in fact, bore little resemblance to the regular companies that existed outside London at that time. In those days, the main function of such was to support visiting stars. Until the coming of the railways, it was quite impractical for supporting companies to accompany the leading actors of the London stage on their provincial tours and these performers had to rely on local casts. This led to the growth of what became known as the 'stock system'.

Under the stock system, actors would be employed to perform specific functions, or 'lines of business' as they were called. There would be a leading man, a leading lady, a comedian, an old man, an old woman etc., a whole range of functions all the way from the tragedian, who was usually the highest paid, to the general utility actors, who received very little. When the visiting star arrived, there was often no time for rehearsal, so all these actors had to be thoroughly experienced in their respective functions and well-versed in the plays they were to perform. Although this form of theatre company certainly had its uses—in the absence of drama schools, for instance, it provided an opportunity for novice actors to enter the profession—the system inevitably led to a restricted repertoire and a somewhat mechanical style of performance.

The Edinburgh Theatre Royal company, although it was certainly capable of fulfilling the stock functions when required, was never a stock company as such. This was wholly due to the nature of the theatre's business. The annual season, which did not include visiting attractions, ran for 35 weeks of the year, involving a repertoire of up to two dozen plays. To sustain such a season required actors of a very high calibre, possessing versatility as well as talent.

Since such actors are always in short supply, it is not surprising that Murray was always at great pains to ensure that the best of them remained in Edinburgh. Although the salaries the actors received were not particularly high, he always made sure that they were paid regularly—by no means a common occurrence among theatre managers of the time!—and he was fairly generous in allowing the theatre to be used for benefit performances. As a result, Murray generally succeeded in retaining the loyalty of his actors, many of whom remained in his service for the best part of their working lives.

Such an actor was Charles Mackay, the undisputed star of the Theatre Royal, who remained with Murray for 22 years. At the height of his popularity, Mackay was paid just £4 per week, supplemented by seasonal benefits which would bring in perhaps another £200. This was excellent money for the time, no doubt, but it was hardly commensurate with Mackay's great appeal and a less perceptive man might have been tempted to look elsewhere. Mackay, however, never faltered in his loyalty to Murray, and this loyalty was reciprocated by the manager. Benson Hill, a small-part actor who was in the company for a few seasons in the 1820s, tells the following story, which amply demonstrates the nature of this loyalty and throws some light on the characters of both men.

> While Mackay and I were on the stage, some drunkards in the boxes threw oranges— I imagined at me, for my companion was an established favourite. I, however, bowed and continued to face the pelters. Their next aim was unmistakably at Mackay. He stood firm as a millstone and *thanked the gentlemen*, in tones of ginger-grating scorn. We had heard a brief, abrupt exclamation behind the scenes; we now *saw*, and the offenders *felt*, its cause. Thump! Whack! By the blood of the Murrays, our zealous little manager had rushed up to the disgraced part of his Theatre, and vigorously flooring these unprovoked ruffians, had them carried off to durance vile...

Mackay, who was described by a contemporary as a 'warm little man', seems to have worn his celebrity well and never lost his popularity with Scottish audiences. He was born in the Lawnmarket in 1787, but moved to Glasgow at the age of nine when his father, a saddler, set up in business there. After a spell in the army, he made his stage debut sometime around 1815. His wife Jeannie was also on the stage—she played small parts with the company—and his son, Hector, later made a stage career in America.

Although he was wise enough to be aware of his limitations as an actor, Mackay would happily attempt any rôle he was given to play; his non-Waverley parts included the First Witch in *Macbeth*, Touchstone in *As You Like It* and Colonel Hardy in John Poole's *Paul Pry*. Critics may have been divided on the quality of his performance in such rôles, but they all agreed that in the Waverley dramas he was inimitable. As we have seen, it was Mackay's portrayal of Bailie Nicol Jarvie in *Rob Roy* which initiated the Theatre Royal's success, and over the years he would bring to life a whole range of Scott characters: Dominie Sampson, Edie Ochiltree, Caleb Balderstone, Dugald Dalgetty, Richie Moniplies and the Laird of Dumbiedykes. His success in these rôles created a tradition in comedy acting and, in fact, added a new phrase to the language. Although he had a host of imitators, he himself was 'the real Mackay'.

These performances, not surprisingly, delighted Sir Walter, who never missed any opportunity to pay tribute to Mackay's talent. As a matter of fact, on that famous occasion—mentioned in the previous chapter—when Scott publicly admitted his authorship of the Waverley Novels, it was while making a toast to Mackay that the admission was made.

> I beg leave to propose the health of my friend, Bailie Nicol Jarvie. And I am sure that when the author of *Waverley* and *Rob Roy* drinks to Nicol Jarvie, it will be received with the just applause to which that gentleman has always been accustomed...

Three years earlier, however, Scott had honoured Mackay in a rather more creative manner. On the opening night of *St Ronan's Well* in 1824, Mackay had agreed 'for one night only' to attempt the character of Meg Dods, the waspish landlady of the Cleikum Inn. Although Scott, as usual, had had little to do with the adaptation—which was by J R Planché—he did write an epilogue for Mackay to speak in character at the end of the evening. This epilogue was to become Mackay's 'party piece' which he would use frequently over the years, whenever he was called upon to give a solo performance. The last three verses read as follows:

> I came a piece frae west o' Curry;
> And, since I see ye're in a hurry,
> Your patience I'll nae langer worry,
>   But be sae crouse
> As speak a word for ane Will Murray
>   That keeps this house.
>
> Plays are auld-fashioned things, in truth,
> And ye've seen wonders mair uncouth;
> Yet actors shouldna suffer drouth
>   Or want of dramock,
> Although they speak but wi' their mouth
>   No with their stamock.
>
> Weill, sirs, guid-een and have a care.
> The bairns make fun o' Meg nae mair;
> For, gin they do, she tells ye fair
>   And without failzie,
> As sure as ever ye sit there,
>   *She'll tell the Bailie!*

Scott's connection with the company was, of course, of enormous importance. Besides writing novels that proved an almost inexhaustible source for the repertoire, Scott used his considerable influence to enhance the company's reputation, acting as a kind of unofficial public relations officer for the Theatre Royal. It was Scott, for instance, who arranged for the company to give a Command Performance—the first ever in Scotland—during the Royal Visit of George IV in 1822. Since the cast of *Rob Roy* on that evening included many who would make lasting contributions to the life of the Theatre Royal, it would be as well to consider it in some detail.

The part of Rob was played by J W Calcraft, a former army officer who, like Mackay, took up the stage after the conclusion of his military service. Calcraft (whose real name was Cole) joined the company in 1818 and remained for six years before departing to go into management in Dublin. As an actor, he had a very broad range, his parts including Sir Brian de Bois Guilbert in *Ivanhoe*, Iago in *Othello* (which he once played with the visiting Edmund Kean) and Dandie Dinmont in *Guy Mannering*. In addition to his acting, however, he was extremely useful as an adaptor of plays and was responsible for a number of Waverley Dramas, his most successful adaptation being *The Bride of Lammermoor*. This was first produced in 1821 and became very popular, enjoying many revivals over the next fifty years.

The part of the villain, Rashleigh Osbaldistone, was played by Edward Denham, a young Borderer who had actually been discovered by Calcraft. During a visit to Kelso, Calcraft found Denham playing with a group of strolling players and immediately introduced him to Murray, who took the young man on at a very small salary. Denham, however, quickly established himself as a Theatre Royal regular and seemed particularly adept at playing Scottish aristocrats. His most famous rôle was that of King James in *George Heriot* (based on *The Fortunes of Nigel*), which Denham first played in 1823. According to Calcraft, writing in the *Dublin University Magazine* many years later, this performance delighted Sir Walter Scott almost as much as Mackay's Bailie had done.

> It was unique, one of those unexpected coincidences you never dream of, and greatly assisted by a natural thickness of utterance, a sort of Border burr (which Sir Walter Scott himself had), in exact keeping with the physical pecularities of the British Solomon.

This performance undoubtedly helped make *George Heriot* one of the most popular of all the Waverley Dramas. Denham, a big burly man—who had, by a curious coincidence, been educated at George Heriot's school in Edinburgh—remained with the company for the next seven years, until his sudden death at the age of 29 in 1830. As far as can be established, apart from summer performances in Perth and Glasgow, he never acted anywhere else.

This cannot be said of another member of the cast, Albert Duff, who played Dougal. Duff, a native of Edinburgh, was a long-standing member of the company, having first been employed by Siddons in 1809. He was a character actor of some ability who won the respect and admiration of his peers but, unfortunately, his story is one that is all too common in the annals of stage history—although, in this case, it was to have a fairly happy ending. After leaving Edinburgh in 1825 to take up an engagement at the Haymarket in London, Duff's love of the bottle all but destroyed him. Six years later, Calcraft paid a visit to London to recruit a new company and found him living in squalor. The Dublin manager immediately took his old friend under his wing and brought him to Ireland, where he remained for the rest of his days as a valued member of Calcraft's company.

Before considering some of the female members of the cast, mention should be made of one actor who, although not actually on the stage that night, was certainly present. This was the theatre prompter, Alexander Bell, known to all and sundry simply as 'Sandy'. Sandy had played the smallish part of Andrew Fairservice in the original production of *Rob Roy* but, this being a royal occasion, Murray replaced him with the more experienced James Aiken. Sandy was never to know any kind of personal fame as an actor, but he was very well-liked

Jane Renaud as Douglas by S de Wilde
Courtesy of the Garrick Club

by the Theatre Royal audience. (As a matter of fact, on the occasions when he did appear, his billing was never 'Mr Bell' but always simply 'Sandy'). Fame did not entirely elude him, however, for it was discovered in his posterity. Sandy was the great-grandfather of Alexander Graham Bell, the inventor of the telephone.

The most senior actress in the cast was Jane Renaud, who played Helen MacGregor. Mrs Renaud had a long association with the Edinburgh stage, going back to 1808, when she first appeared in the city during a short season under the management of Robert William Elliston. At that time she was known as Mrs Powell, being married to an actor of that name, and played Lady Macbeth and Julia in *The Rivals*. Ten years later, having spent some years in the Haymarket company, she divorced Powell, married Renaud (who was not an actor, but a tailor) and returned to Edinburgh to join the Theatre Royal company, where she remained until her retiral in 1829.

Jane Renaud was what was known in those days as a 'heavy woman'—that is to say, she played women of substance rather than helpless heroines or sweet young things. Her first part under Murray's management was Lady Randolph in Home's *Douglas* and, for her benefit, she gave a performance of *Hamlet*—one of the first actresses in history to attempt the rôle. Her most memorable performances, however, came in Waverley Dramas; besides Helen, these included Meg Merrilees in *Guy Mannering*, Alice Gray in *The Bride of Lammermoor*, Janet of Tomahourick in *Twa Drovers* and Queen Caroline in *The Heart of Midlothian*. She was a very physical actress, whose power was said to have been comparable to that of Sarah Siddons. This probably accounts for her very long career, which began in London in 1787, when she made her debut as Alicia in Nicholas Rowe's *Jane Shore*. By the time she said her farewell to the Theatre Royal audience, therefore, she had been playing featured rôles for 42 years.

In the cast that evening, however, was a group of actresses whose combined careers lasted for an even longer period of time. These were the Nicols, a family of Edinburgh actors whose presence at the Theatre Royal would last for more than 50 years. On the night in question, the part of Jean MacAlpine was played by Sarah Nicol, Mattie by her eldest daughter Emma, and the very small part of Martha by nine-year old Julia.

Twenty years earlier, Sarah Bezra, a young woman of mixed Irish-Hungarian descent, had been employed as a domestic servant in the household of a certain Colonel Milner in London. Her passion for the stage led to her secret membership of an amateur dramatic club and, when she was inevitably discovered in this, she fully expected to be discharged. Fortunately for Sarah, however, Mrs Milner was understanding of her ambition, allowed her to retain the job and arranged for her to have some acting lessons. She did not, however, make her professional debut until after her marriage to Nicol, who was an Edinburgh printer. This was in an obscure and long-forgotten play called *Valentine and Orson*, produced in 1806 under the management of a Mr Aickin. She remained in the company for another 28 years, until her retirement in 1834, becoming famous for her 'old woman' rôles. Besides Jean MacAlpine, she was Mrs Flockhart in *Waverley*, Mrs McTavish in Murray's *Gilderoy*, Mrs Suddlechop in *George Heriot* and Mrs Malaprop in *The Rivals*.

Mrs Nicol had three daughters, all of whom became performers. The youngest, Maria, had a very sweet voice and became very popular as a concert singer. Although she appeared at the Theatre Royal in small parts as a child, she concentrated on her singing as she grew older and was only seen at the Theatre Royal when a vocalist was required. The middle sister, Julia, was very much an actress and became a popular leading lady on the Northern Circuit—of which more later—playing rôles such as Ellen in *The Lady of the Lake* and Catherine Glover in *The Fair Maid of Perth*. She was apparently very beautiful and the most famous rôle of her youth was that of Mary, Queen of Scots in Murray's play, *Mary Stuart*. As she grew older, she began to excel in heavier rôles and her Helen MacGregor, which she played first in Glasgow in 1840, won particular praise.

The most interesting Nicol of all, however, was Sarah's first child, Emma, whose stage career lasted for 50 years. Emma joined the company in 1812 as a child actress and, by 1822, was playing substantial rôles: Maria in *Twelfth Night*, Miss Neville in *She Stoops to Conquer* and, most famously, Madge Wildfire in *The Heart of Midlothian*. In 1826, however, she left the company to take up an engagement at Drury Lane and did not return for another seven years. Her movements during this time are unknown, but one assumes she was playing in London and the English provinces. In 1834, on her mother's retiral from the stage, she returned to Edinburgh and immediately began to play Sarah's parts. She was so successful in replicating her mother's performances that it was said that many of the Theatre Royal audience never knew the difference. Emma Nicol remained with the company for the rest of her working life, which would outlast that of the Theatre Royal itself.

The most important—and perhaps the most intriguing—actress in the cast was the manager's sister, who played the part of Diana Vernon. Although she was often described as 'Edinburgh's own Mrs Siddons', this says more about the publicity value of the Siddons name than it does about Harriet's acting. The fact is that the former Miss Murray had a quality which was quite different from that of her mother-in-law. She was not a 'heavy woman' but rather one who was best seen, in the words of her friend and cousin-through-marriage Fanny Kemble, 'in parts that called for her own qualities of grace, goodness and beauty'.

Seven years older than her brother, Harriet Murray made her debut at the age of ten, playing Prince Arthur in a production of *Henry VIII*. As she grew older, she played a succession of leading rôles, first in Bristol and Bath, later at Covent Garden. By the time she was 17, she had become established as one of the most popular leading ladies on the London Stage. In 1800, the *Authentic Memoirs of the Green Room* described her thus.

> This charming actress gains upon the public favour with each repeated performance. In scenes which require the felicitous union of pathos with simplicity—a walk, perhaps, as arduous as any in the whole range of the drama—Miss Murray is superior. She sings, likewise, with considerable taste; her voice is uncommonly soft and pleasing, especially in plaintive airs, which she executes with a degree of feeling and simplicity...

Over the next nine years, Harriet continued to play leading rôles on the London stage, at both Covent Garden and Drury Lane, where her parts included Rosalind, Desdemona, Viola, and Juliet. Shortly after her arrival in Edinburgh, she played Ophelia to her husband's Hamlet and later added Portia to her Shakespearian repertoire.

As an actress, therefore, there can be no doubt about the abilities of Harriet Siddons and it seems somewhat unfortunate that her reputation should suffer by this rather empty comparison with her mother-in-law. It is the part that she played in the management of the Theatre Royal, however, that gives most cause for speculation.

When Henry Siddons had first secured the Patent in 1809, he decided that, rather than spending money on the Theatre Royal, he would take a lease on the Leith Walk theatre and concentrate his energies there. The reasons for doing this—which involved considerable expense—are unclear, but of rather more importance is the question of Harriet's involvement in the decision. Ever since their marriage in 1802, Harriet and Henry had worked together and it is reasonable to assume that they took such decisions jointly.

After the death of Siddons, however, the rôle that Harriet played seems much more vague. From the available records, it is clear that she left the day-to-day running of the theatre to William, but the nature of their business relationship is undetermined. The formalities of the time, unfortunately, do not help us here, for a sense of old-fashioned courtesy imbued all such relationships. For instance, the first management decision to be taken after the death of Siddons was the raising of the price of the boxes. Murray explained this decision in a public statement, the wording of which clearly indicates that this was a decision he had taken alone. Harriet may or may not have been privy to this but, if she was, it would have been considered ungallant for Murray even to suggest as much.

On the other hand, it *was* suggested on one occasion—by a hostile critic in the *Dramatic Review*—that William Murray was simply his sister's servant and could do nothing without her approval. Although, from all that is known of Murray, this seems most unlikely, the fact is that Harriet Siddons was the sole proprietor of the Theatre Royal and, until 1829, the holder of the Patent. In other words, it was she who held the power and on one occasion at least—to be explored in the next chapter—she did not hesitate to use it.

For the most part, however, she seemed content to concentrate on her acting and to defer to her brother in all business matters. As a matter of fact, there is only one instance in which she was seen to have taken any kind of theatrical initiative. This was in 1819 when, on a visit to London, she saw Tom Dibdin's *The Heart of Midlothian* at the Surrey Theatre and immediately set about acquiring the play for Edinburgh. This was produced with great success, the *Scotsman* declaring that Mrs Siddons, in the part of Jeannie Deans, produced 'something quite above the ordinary line of acting'.

Harriet Siddons was a small woman, with fine, sensitive features. On her retiral from the stage in 1830, it was said of her, again by the *Scotsman*, that 'no one ever succeeded so thoroughly in giving to the stage the air of the drawing-room'. When she died in the November of 1844, her brother was so deeply affected that he did not appear on the Theatre Royal stage for another six months.

The Royal Command Performance, in which all of the above took part, was not only a glittering theatrical occasion but an important milestone in the company's fortunes. It was at this precise moment that the Theatre Royal gained the reputation that was described in the previous chapter. One consequence of this was that leading London actors began to appear in Edinburgh, not as visiting attractions but as members of the regular company.

Perhaps the best example of this was John Vandenhoff, a former schoolmaster of Dutch extraction who was one of the leading tragedians of his time. Vandenhoff made his debut at Covent Garden in 1820 and played regularly in London for the rest of his life. He was best known for his playing of the title rôle of *Coriolanus* and the part of Creon in the *Antigone* of Sophocles. In 1823, Vandenhoff joined the Theatre Royal and remained a member of the company

BY COMMAND
OF

HIS MAJESTY.

This present Evening, TUESDAY, August 27. 1822,

Will be performed the National Opera of

ROB ROY MACGREGOR,
OR
AULD LANGSYNE.

WITH THE ORIGINAL MUSIC, AND APPROPRIATE SCENERY, MACHINERY, DRESSES AND DECORATIONS.

Sir Frederick Vernon by Mr MUNRO,
Rashleigh Osbaldiston by Mr DENHAM—Francis Osbaldiston by Mr HUCKEL,
Captain Thornton by Mr MURRAY—Major Galbraith by Mr WEEKES,
Rob Roy Macgregor Campbell by Mr CALCRAFT,
Bailie Nicol Jarvie by Mr MACKAY,
Mr Owen by Mr ROBERTS—MacStewart by Mr LEE—Dougal by Mr DUFF.
Willie by Master HILLYARD—Andrew by Mr AIKIN—Lancie by Mr STANLEY,
Sergeant by Mr HILLYARD—Saunders Wylie by Mr POWER,
Highlanders by Messrs Broadhurst, Sandilands, Robertson, Hewson, Cameron, Plover, Merryck, Glegg, Norman, &c. &c.
Travellers by Messrs Field, Lylesford, Brodie, Dunstable, Eccles, Fotheringham, Gessner, Kerry, Larder, Stormount, &c.
Lennox Troopers by Messrs Grant, Heath, Thomson, Reid, Chisholm, Robb, and Rutherford,
English Soldiers by Messrs Lawson, Lorimer, Reinard, Charteris, Belsham, Orrock, Blenheim, Burgess, Lennox, Cross, &c.
Helen Macgregor by Mrs RENAUD,
Martha by Miss J. NICOL—Mattie by Miss NICOL—Hostess by Mrs MACKAY—Jean M'Alpine by Mrs NICOL,
Diana Vernon, for this Night only, by Mrs H. SIDDONS.

THE SCENERY WILL BE EXHIBITED IN THE FOLLOWING SUCCESSION:

ACT THE FIRST.	ACT THE SECOND.
1. INTERIOR OF VILLAGE INN.	1. THE COLLEGE GARDENS OF GLASGOW,
LIBRARY IN OSBALDISTON HALL.	AND VIEW OF THE SPIRE OF ST MUNGO.
3. ROOM IN BAILIE NICOL JARVIE'S.	2. LIBRARY IN OSBALDISTON HALL.
4. THE OLD BRIDGE OF GLASGOW.	3. INTERIOR OF JEAN M'ALPINE'S CHANGE HOUSE.
5. HALL IN GLASGOW TOLBOOTH.	4. THE CLACHAN OF ABERFOYLE,
6. CELL IN THE TOLBOOTH OF GLASGOW.	AND DISTANT VIEW OF THE HIGHLAND LOCH.

ACT THE THIRD.

1. THE PASS OF LOCHARD.	3. INTERIOR OF JEAN M'ALPINE'S CHANGE HOUSE.
2. ROMANTIC GLEN IN THE HIGHLANDS.	4. VIEW OF LOCHLOMOND, MOONLIGHT.

No Free Admission can be granted on the present Occasion, Renters and Subscribers to the Theatre excepted.

The Pit and Gallery Doors will this Evening Open at Six o'Clock—The Box Door will Open at half past Six precisely; and the Time appointed for the Commencement of the Performances is Eight o'Clock—It is therefore most earnestly and respectfully requested, that Ladies and Gentlemen will be early in their Attendance.

The Transfer Office will not be Opened this Evening, as, the moment that the Pit and Galleries are filled, Placards will be issued, notifying the same, and should any Lady or Gentleman taking a Ticket for the Pit be too late in securing Admittance, their Money will be returned on Production of the Ticket To-Morrow Morning, at the Box-Office.

No Money will be taken at the Box Entrance until the Tickets issued for this Evening are received.

All Carriages will set down with the Horses' Heads towards Waterloo Place, and take up in the Opposite Direction.

To-Morrow the Tragedy of OTHELLO—the Character of *Othello* by Mr KEAN.
It being his Last Appearance here but Three this Season.

VIVAT REX.

Theatre Royal: Command Performance for George IV, 1822

for more than a decade. Between 1823 and 1834, Vandenhoff would spend the winter in Edinburgh and return to London in the spring. Other actors who followed this practice included Frederick Yates, Charles Kemble and, of course, Scott's friend and adaptor, Daniel Terry.

At the same time, of course, the company provided early experience for many actors who would later become famous in London and elsewhere. Almost inevitably, therefore, as the years passed, the purely Scottish dimension of the theatre's work—in terms of both personnel and repertoire—tended to become less and less prominent, particularly after the death of Sir Walter Scott in 1832. The company retained its own unique character, however, and in 1829 increased in size.

In that year, the Patent that had been granted to Henry Siddons twenty years earlier came up for renewal. Harriet Siddons, having decided to retire, urged her brother to become the new Patent holder and, after some hesitation—he had apparently received a rather tempting offer to act at Covent Garden—Murray agreed.

His first act as Patentee was to contact James Black, a Leith businessman who was the major shareholder in the Caledonian Theatre. Murray made a bargain with Black to take out a long-term lease on the Caledonian, which he immediately re-named the Adelphi. By skilfully arranging his seasons—playing the Theatre Royal in the winter and the Adelphi in the summer— he ran both theatres successfully for the next 20 years.

This gave Murray a monopoly of theatre production in Edinburgh, which did not come to an end until 1843, when the Theatres Act was repealed and a period of free trade introduced. Murray protested against this measure vehemently, not because he was opposed to free trade but because he felt that the Government were betraying the bargain they had struck with him as the Patent holder. Dashing off a letter to his MP, Sir George Clark, Murray argued that legislation should be postponed until all existing Patents had expired. When this happened, he declared, the Government

> ...might fairly make any change in the law which may be deemed adequate, but surely no injury should be done to those who have induced themselves liable in heavy debts and made considerable outlays in the faith of the Patent granted them.

It was a matter of principle as far as Murray was concerned. His Patent was supposed to run for 20 years, not 13, and he considered that the Goverment was breaking faith with him. He cannot seriously have thought that the new law would harm his business, for Edinburgh could not possibly support more than two theatres of the size of the Theatre Royal and the Adelphi. In the event, no serious competitor emerged and Murray's monopoly remained intact.

The acquistion of a second house, however, had another consequence. With an eye to the future, Murray had already begun to encourage some of the younger members of the company to take an interest in management. Now, with two theatres to run, he had the opportunity to give some practical instruction through the obvious need to delegate some of the work. His two most favoured assistants at this time were H F Lloyd and Montague Stanley.

Stanley is possibly the more interesting of the two. A Dundonian by birth, he was the son of a naval officer and spent some years in Canada and Jamaica as a child. When he made his professional debut at York in 1824, he used the stage name of 'Manby' but when he joined the Theatre Royal company in 1826, he reverted to his family name. He was a light leading man, excelling in such rôles as Francis Osbaldistone in *Rob Roy* and Robin in *The Twa Drovers*. His talents were not restricted to his acting, however, and he was a fine singer, an expert swordsman, a landscape painter of some reputation and a serious poet. Apart from three years in London—during which he acted with the Drury Lane company—he spent his entire career at the Theatre Royal. This career came to an end under somewhat unusual circumstances. In 1838, Stanley had some kind of religious conversion, which led him to decide that it would be wrong for him to continue as an actor. He then devoted himself almost entirely to his painting and was elected an associate of the Royal Scottish Academy in 1839. He bought a house on the island of Bute, where he died of consumption in 1844. According to all who knew him, he had a gentle, compassionate nature, although he was something of a solitary and mixed little with the other members of the company. As an actor, his performances were said to be invariably intelligent, if somewhat cold and deficient of feeling.

H F Lloyd, who was Murray's assistant for almost 20 years, was a completely different character. Lloyd, who came from Exeter, made his Edinburgh debut in 1829, when he played the Caledonian, then under the management of Charles Bass. Three years later, he was invited to join the Theatre Royal company and he remained with Murray until 1848, when he left to join the management of the Prince's Theatre in Glasgow. Three years later, he returned to take over the Theatre Royal's management on Murray's retiral.

Lloyd was what known in these days as a 'low comedian' and enjoyed great popularity as such. As a matter of fact, his popularity is said to have matched that of Mackay, although Lloyd was a very different kind of actor. Mackay was a 'legitimate' comedian, his function being to bring humourous relief to what was an essentially dramatic situation. Lloyd, on the other hand, was a clown and a farceur, his characters having names like 'Malty', 'Jacques Strop' and 'Benjamin Bowbell'. In 1849, the *Dramatic Omnibus* published an article about him which praised his talent highly.

> We must decidedly say that his is, in our opinion, the most naturally funny low comedian we know. There is an oiliness and an unction about his humour, which we look for in vain from his more artistic and studied contemporaries. There seems to be no effort whatever in his racy humour, it flows almost uncalled for, and keeps one in roars of laughter whether they will or no.

The *Dramatic Omnibus* was quite wrong about this apparent lack of effort, for Lloyd was a painstaking perfectionist who worked very hard at being funny. In his old age, he told the readers of a Glasgow newspaper that 'I was never thoroughly satisfied with my acting at any part of my life'.

Despite his success as an actor—and despite Murray's tuition—Lloyd did not fare well in management, only surviving at the Theatre Royal for a single season, after which he was obliged to take refuge in the debtor's sanctuary at Holyrood. This failure was, no doubt, largely due to Lloyd's own shortcomings, but it is only fair to point out that he had at least one problem with which Murray never had to contend. Not far away—practically across the road—the Adelphi now provided competition and was, furthermore, in the hands of one of the most effective theatre managers of his time.

Robert Wyndham, who came from Salisbury, had began his career as member of Macready's company at Covent Garden and had first come to Scotland to play at the Adelphi in Glasgow, then under the management of David Prince Miller. Murray had seen him acting there and, impressed by Wyndham's versatility, offered him a job in Edinburgh. He was to be Murray's last assistant and took over the management of the Adelphi on Murray's retirement. As an actor, Wyndham never failed to shine in anything he was given to play, whether it was tragedy, farce, National Drama or the classics. It was as a manager, however, that he would win lasting fame. At the Adelphi at that time, Wyndham was laying the foundations of a theatrical empire, which would be the inheritance of his son Fred and his partner, J B Howard.

Fred Wyndham, however, very nearly did not live to collect this inheritance. On the evening of 24 May, 1853, there was some kind of accident with the gas fire in the musician's room at the Adelphi, resulting in a conflagration that destroyed the building completely. The manager's house being above the theatre, Mrs Wyndham and Fred (who was less than a week old at the time) had to be rescued by the fire brigade. This, the first fire ever to occur in an Edinburgh theatre, proved to be a mixed blessing. Black and his partners, who owned the Adelphi, had been thinking of pulling it down and building a new theatre—the fire saved them the trouble. As for Wyndham, he simply moved his company into the Theatre Royal, which was standing vacant at the time.

He was still there seven years later, when the history of the Theatre Royal finally came to an end. The Goverment, requiring a site for the new General Post Office, acquired the property by compulsory purchase for a price of £30,000. By this time, of course, the Adephi had been rebuilt and Wyndham was running both theatres. It fell to Wyndham, therefore, to organise the last Gala evening of the old Theatre Royal.

This took place on 25 May, 1859, the programme reflecting past, present and future concerns. Most of the actors mentioned in this chapter were no more, but ways were found to remember them in spirit. Murray was represented by a performance of *Cramond Brig*, the one-act curtain-raiser he had written for the Royal Command Performance. Scenes from *Rob Roy* were played and although there was no Mackay, the part of the Bailie was played by George Webster, the latest inheritor of the tradition of Scottish comedy-acting that Mackay had initiated. The sole survivor from the cast of the Command Performance—'the last rose of summer' Wyndham called her—was Miss Emma Nicol.

The main play of the evening was a contemporary piece: Tom Taylor's *Masks and Faces*. In the cast that evening was John Vandenhoff, who had come out of retirement for the occasion; Edmund Glover—whose career will be discussed in a later chapter—of the Glasgow Theatre Royal; and a young, somewhat gauche, albeit enthusiastic young man whom Wyndham had been bringing on and who would, in the years to come, write a glorious page in the history of the English theatre: Henry Irving.

It was, as they say, the end of an era. For half a century, the Edinburgh Theatre Royal had stood as a beacon of excellence that inspired theatrical activity all over Scotland, creating a precedent that would never be completely forgotten. After that night, however, it soon became clear that something important had vanished from Scottish theatrical life.

The company moved into the Adelphi, which was immediately re-named the Theatre Royal, and in the years immediately following, Wyndham would make it over into the finest stock company in the British Isles—yet it was a stock company for all of that. Although he was never indifferent to Scottish aspirations, frequently staged the Waverley Dramas and, in fact, encouraged the writing and production of new Scottish plays, Wyndham remained at heart what Murray had never been—an English provincial manager. Even if he had been more like Murray, however, it would probably have made no difference. The Scottish theatrical indentity was about to be engulfed by a tidal wave of change which would come close to extinguishing it completely. Mercifully, its survival did not depend on the fortunes of any single theatre or company. If we consider the wider theatrical context in which the Theatre Royal was pre-eminent, we will find that, in other parts of Scotland, other developments were taking place. These developments would not only ensure survival but would, in time, lead to a renewal of the Scottish theatrical voice.

Chapter Five

LADY MACBETH OF ABERDEEN

No other Scottish city—not even Edinburgh—has a longer dramatic history than Aberdeen. In the Middle Ages it was famous for its pageants and mystery plays, conducted under the supervision of two city officials known as 'The Abbot and Prior of Bon Accord'. As a matter of fact, the earliest known production of any play in Scotland—a morality entitled *The Halie Blude*—took place in Aberdeen in the year 1440. In 1562, when Mary, Queen of Scots visited the city, she was greeted by all manner of plays, spectacles and interludes which had been specifically devised for her entertainment. As late as 1601, a company of English comedians—William Shakespeare, it is said, among them—played a season in Aberdeen under the management of Lawrence Fletcher.

In the aftermath of the Reformation, however, opposition to the theatre was more bitter and unrelenting in Aberdeen than it was anywhere else. In Aberdeen, it was not simply a matter of the ministers putting pressure on the magistrates to restrict theatrical activity: on this matter, the Aberdeen ministers and magistrates were at one. They simply refused to allow actors to play in the city. In 1751, for instance, Sarah Ward and some actors from the Taylor's Hall in Edinburgh attempted to play a season in Aberdeen—and found that they were not even allowed within the city walls. In 1768, an actor-manager called William Fisher fared little better. He managed to fit up a theatre in Shoe Lane, only to find himself closed down as soon as he opened for business. It was not until 1779 that the Aberdeen establishment was finally persuaded to permit any company of actors to perform in the city. In that year, the Shoe Lane theatre was taken over by a man whose name figures prominently in the affairs of the Scottish Theatre during this period: John Jackson.

The son of a Yorkshire clergyman, Jackson had been educated for the Church, but family troubles forced him to give up any hopes he may have had in that direction. Deciding on an acting career, he made his debut in 1762 in the title rôle of *Oronooko* (an adaptation by Thomas Southerne of the novel by Aphra

Behn) at the Canongate Playhouse in Edinburgh. He was successful enough, in this and other rôles, to be engaged by David Garrick at Drury Lane and he remained in London for the next seven years, playing at both Drury Lane and the Haymarket. In 1769, he married the Irish actress Hester Brown, with whom he formed a touring company, and for the next decade the Jacksons were more or less strolling players, travelling all over the British Isles. The move into management had been made, presumably, out of a wish to lead a more regular life.

It has to be said that, as a theatrical artist, Jackson fell some way short of the first rank. His acting, even at its best, was criticised for stiffness of gesture and (a most damning criticism in those days) weakness of voice. His attempts at dramatic authorship—he wrote several plays—met with no success whatsoever. ('Of Jackson's capacity as an author' wrote James Dibdin in his *Annals of the Edinburgh Stage* 'it is perhaps best to say nothing.') Even as a producer of plays, he appears to have had shortcomings, although these can possibly be accounted for by the fact that he did not always have the best talent at his disposal. George Colman the Younger, the distinguished manager of the Haymarket, for whom Jackson had worked in his London days, saw one of Jackson's productions on a visit to Edinburgh and recalled the experience later in his *Random Memories*. 'Few of the company' wrote Colman disdainfully 'rose above the level of mediocrity and most of them failed to reach it.'

Jackson had the qualities of a businessman rather than those of an artist. By juggling the resources of his many theatres, creating an audience where none existed, keeping an eye open for the main chance and by refusing, with the greatest of resolution, ever to admit defeat, he succeeded in remaining in business for the best part of 20 years. The greatest achievement of his career was his survival.

Jackson's ambition, quite clearly, was to establish a circuit that would encompass the whole of Scotland. This was made possible by the statute of 1788 which—as described in Chapter Two—permitted certain 'places of resort' to enjoy short theatrical seasons. In 1781, Jackson had purchased the Theatre Royal in Edinburgh and it was probably the fact that he was the proprietor of the only legal theatre in Scotland that enabled him to operate such seasons in Carlisle, Dumfries, Glasgow, Dundee and Aberdeen. When one considers the degree of hostility that Jackson had to face—not to mention the horrendously primitive transport facilities that he and his company had to use—one is forced to conclude that he must have been a man of prodigious energy and boundless optimism.

He was certainly very optimistic about Aberdeen. After his initial success in Shoe Lane, he decided to build a new theatre in Marischal Street. Unfortunately, almost as soon as work was begun on this project, Jackson became bankrupt and the building stood unfinished for a number of years. Then, in 1795, Stephen Kemble persuaded a number of local merchants to form a syndicate that would enable the building to be completed and fitted up as a theatre. Kemble, who had by this time succeeded Jackson at the Edinburgh Theatre Royal, ran short seasons at Aberdeen in tandem with his Edinburgh enterprise until 1800 when he, too, ran into financial difficulties. The theatre continued under several undistinguished managers for the next few years until 1812, when the syndicate, having grown weary of what must have seemed to them to be a white elephant, decided to put the place up for sale by public roup. Before such an auction could take place, however, the theatre was purchased outright by an Aberdeen merchant called John Fraser.

Fraser's interest in making this purchase can only be guessed at. Presumably he had bought the place purely as a business venture, for he had no theatrical background and his first act was to engage a manager. On the other hand, he did have a stage-struck daughter and it may have been at her urging that Fraser was persuaded to make the purchase. It is certainly the case that, for the rest of her life, Jessie Fraser always proved most adept at getting other people to do what she wanted.

The man that Fraser hired to run the Marischal Street house was a bred-in-the-bone provincial actor called Corbet Ryder. Born in 1780, Ryder was a member of the large family—believed to have been Welsh in origin—of a well-known manager on the West of England circuit, Preswick Ryder. In his youth he had shown promise enough to gain a place with the Drury Lane company, but he did not remain in London for more than a couple of seasons. In 1804, he was in Yorkshire, acting at Richmond and Harrogate, and it was at this time that he married the actress Louisa Goldfinch. Between then and his arrival in Aberdeen, his movements are unknown and all that can be reasonably assumed is that, at some point during this period in Corbet Ryder's life, Louisa Ryder died. Very shortly after his arrival in Aberdeen, Corbet Ryder married Jessie Fraser.

At the time, he was 32 years of age, a widower with two young children to bring up: a little girl called Peggy and his only son, Tom, who was just a baby at the time. Jessie was only 15 years old but lost no time in creating a new family. Apart from mothering Peggy and Tom, she quickly presented Corbet with twin girls, Jessie and Emma. In time, all four Ryder children would become members of a company which would barnstorm its way around Scotland for more than 30 years. What came to be known as 'the Northern Circuit' was very much the creation of the Ryder family.

In order to explain the growth of this circuit, it is necessary to describe the work of a provincial theatre manager in some detail. With such a short theatrical season, the theatre was occupied for most of the year by performances that were not prohibited by the Theatres Act: recitals, concerts, soirées etc. Although it was the manager's responsibility to book such performances in, he could safely leave their administration to a house manager while he took the company off to develop his business elsewhere.

The circuit which Corbet and Jessie Ryder established between the years 1817-24 established a pattern which would last, in one form or another, for roughly the next 50 years. When the season had ended in Aberdeen, they would travel to Perth, where they would perform for the next two months. Initially, performances were given in a little theatre in St Anne's Lane, but such was the popularity of these seasons that a new and larger theatre was soon required. This theatre—illegally styled the Theatre Royal—was erected by public subscription in 1820, on the junction of Atholl Street and Kinnoul Street, the site of the old Blackfriars Monastery.

At the end of June, the Ryder company would leave Perth and play for a few weeks in Montrose. At the beginning of August, they would open in Dundee. The Dundee theatre—also called the Theatre Royal—was situated in Castle Street and during the months of August and September the company would play a season there, in tandem with performances at the Trades Hall, Arbroath. At the end of September, they would return to Aberdeen.

This, at least, was the itinerary at the beginning. As the popularity of the company grew, and an audience developed, the Ryders began to enjoy a more relaxed and easy-going relationship with the various authorities and would often find themselves playing in these towns throughout the year. This was especially the case when Ryder began to book visiting stars. These would only be available for a matter of weeks and, if all the towns were to be covered, performances had to be arranged accordingly. In the late summer of 1820, for instance, William Charles Macready was booked for a three-week engagement, which involved the company playing in Aberdeen, Montrose, Dundee and Perth.

There is, in fact, a rather romantic story attached to that particular engagement. At the time, Macready was 27 years old and at the very beginning of his celebrity. The son of a circuit manager in the North of England, he had originally intended to become a lawyer but had been frustrated in this ambition by his father's bankruptcy and eventual death. In order to support his mother and sister, he was obliged to enter a profession for which he always felt a deep dislike. His reluctance as an actor did not prevent him from making a substantial contribution ot the art of theatre—including the rescue of Shakespeare from the corruption of Restoration dramatists—but it did give him a bad reputation among his fellow professionals. He avoided their company and was known to be arrogant, snobbish and perpetually bad-tempered—although, to be fair to him, these characteristics were, in the main, manifestations of his scrupulous professional perfectionism. This is quite evident in the *Journals* that Macready kept throughout his long acting life, telling us so much about himself and the theatre of his time.

During his engagement with Ryder in 1820, Macready played five leading rôles, including *Macbeth, Richard III, Coriolanus, Romeo and Juliet* and a new play by Sheridan Knowles, *Virginius*. In the Shakespeares, his leading lady was Jessie Ryder and their performance together in *Macbeth* was particularly well received. In the Knowles play, however, Jessie had to give way to another actress: 15 year old Katherine Atkins, the daughter of the scene-painter.

She came an hour before the regular summoms, to go through the scenes of Virginia and receive my instructions. She was dressed in a closely fitting tartan frock which showed off to advantage the perfect symmetry of her sylph-like figure. The beauty of her face was more in its expression than in feature, though no want of loveliness was there. Her rehearsals greatly pleased me, her acting being so much in earnest. There is a native grace in her deportment and every movement, and never were innocence and sensibility more sweetly personified than in her mild look and speaking eyes streaming with unbidden tears.

So wrote Macready in his *Journal* on the evening of that first rehearsal. Quite clearly, this unhappy, unpopular, bad-tempered and disagreeable man was deeply in love, a fact which not only surprised all who knew him but aroused the hostility of his family. Macready's sister, in fact, would not agree to the match unless the unfortunate Miss Atkins gave up the stage and spent some years in Kensington, studying how to be a lady! Luckily for Macready, his feelings were reciprocated and, 1824, he married Katherine. They remained together until her death in 1852 and Macready would return to act on the Aberdeen circuit on a number of occasions throughout the remainder of his professional life.

The success of the company, however, did not depend on visiting stars, but was based on other, less measurable factors: Corbet Ryder's personal charm, the quality of cast and an evenly-balanced programme. Ryder's background and experience had taught him the importance of cultivating local sympathy and, apart from this, he seems to have been genuinely popular, both as an actor and as a man. It was largely due to this popularity, in fact, that the citizens of Perth were persuaded to give so generously for the building of their Theatre Royal.

Apart from this, some of the best actors in Scotland were available at this time of year. The Edinburgh season ended in April and, since Murray usually liked to keep his summers free, many of his actors were only too happy to find employment with Ryder. Charles Mackay, for instance, regularly played with the Ryder company during these years.

The programme for each season was a judicious mixture of Shakespeare, Sheridan, comedy, tragedy and melodrama. An 1817 season, for instance, was fairly typical, including *Richard III, Macbeth, Guy Mannering,* a new comedy entitled *Smiles and Tears*, ending with one of Ryder's favourite plays, *The Forest of Bondy or the Dog of Montargis.* The last named was a 'dog drama', in which the faithful hound—played by Ryder's own trained dog, Dragon—leads searchers to the body of his murdered master, pursues the killers and drags them down by the throat!

Ryder relished this play and usually staged it for his benefit performance. It was soon to be supplanted, however, by another play and a part with which Corbet Ryder would become identified for the rest of his life. This play—once again—was *Rob Roy*, and the story of how it came to find a place in the Ryder repertoire is one that it full of interest.

Scott's novel first appeared in 1817 and its immediate popularity led to a number of adaptations being rushed onto the stage. The first of these was presented at the Leith Walk theatre in Edinburgh, then known as the Pantheon.

Practically nothing is known of this production—which was not a success—but it is at least possible that this was the maladroit version by George Soane, described in Chapter Two. It surely could not have been Isaac Pocock's version, which first took the stage at Covent Garden in March, 1818, with William Charles Macready as Rob and the great English comedian John Liston as Bailie Nicol Jarvie.

This, of course, was the version which would later create such a sensation in Edinburgh. Even so, this success was not anticipated as a foregone conclusion. Perhaps because of the earlier failure of the Pantheon version, Murray was a little wary of Pocock's *Rob Roy* and decided to try it out in Glasgow before committing himself to a production at the Theatre Royal. On this occasion, Bailie Nicol Jarvie was played, not by Mackay, but by Murray himself. If this seems a little surprising, the explanation is quite straightforward. Murray's try-out production took place in June, when Mackay was in Perth, acting with the Ryder company.

As a matter of fact, Mackay very nearly did not play the Bailie even in Perth. Although he had originally been assigned the rôle, another actor in the company demanded that Mackay give it up. This actor, Williams by name, had been acting leading comedy rôles for some time and claimed seniority over Mackay. Ryder offered Mackay the rôle of Rashleigh and, when this was obstinately refused, there was an unholy row. As a result of this, Ryder declared that he had never liked the play in the first place and refused to have anything more to do with it. The fact that the play went on at all was entirely due to the insistence of Jessie, who played Diana Vernon on that occasion. Corbet was most displeased, but rather grudgingly consented to the production going on 'for three nights only' and advertised it as such in the bills. He surrendered the leading rôle—which he, of course, was expected to play—to an actor called Samuel Johnson, and even absented himself from the theatre during the first performance.

This led to a curious misunderstanding which would have a lasting effect on the future of the company. Corbet's father, old Preswick Ryder, was in Perth at the time and had agreed to act as money-taker and to watch the door of the theatre, which meant that he did not actually see the show. He was enough of an old trouper, however, to be able to judge success by the reactions of the audience and, as he heard the rising volume of applause, became convinced that Corbet had made a serious mistake. This applause, of course, was for Mackay—who was playing the part for the very first time—but old Ryder assumed that it was for Johnson. When Corbet eventually returned to the theatre, old Ryder prevailed upon him to get rid of Johnson and take the part of Rob himself. Corbet, on being told how successful the play had been, lost no time in doing this and, as a result, became the most popular Rob Roy of his time. For the next 20 years, Corbet's playing of the rôle would be the mainstay of the company.

The circuit that the Ryders established—the Northern Ciruit as it became known—developed over the years to the point where it became an important feature of Scottish theatrical life. Unfortunately, this development was impeded for a period when, out of a sense of misplaced ambition, the Ryders made a move which they would later come to regret. They gave up summer touring and, instead, took a lease on the Caledonian Theatre in Edinburgh.

The move to Edinburgh was ill-advised for a number of reasons and, in making it, the Ryders gave up every advantage in their possession. On the Northern Circuit, there had been absolutely no competition, whereas in Edinburgh they were practically across the street from the most successful theatre in Scotland. By touring in summer, as we have seen, the Ryders had been able to secure the services of the most capable actors. The Edinburgh seasons, on the other hand, were to take place in the winter, when such actors were simply not available. Lastly, and most importantly, the legal situation had been pretty freely interpreted by the authorities of the northern towns who had, by and large, made the Ryders welcome. In Edinburgh, besides being regarded as impertinent interlopers, their activities were completely illegal.

From all that is known of Corbet Ryder, it seems most unlikely that he was the prime mover in the Edinburgh enterprise. In Rob Lawson's *History of the Scots Stage*, Ryder is described as 'the most astute, kindly and philanthropic manager in the records'—and this was not the act of such a man. Jessie, of course, was made of sterner stuff. When she died in 1875, her obituary in the *Aberdeen Free Press* spoke of her 'singular spirit and energy' and it is highly likely that Ryder was persuaded to take the Caledonian by the urgings of his wife. If this was indeed the case, what followed can be seen as a trial of strength between two determined women: Jessie Ryder and Harriet Siddons.

It is not as if the Ryders were ignorant of the problems that lay ahead. In the summer of 1823, they had added Edinburgh to the company's itinerary, presenting two plays, *Rob Roy* and *Quentin Durward*, at the Caledonian. Almost immediately, they received a letter from Mrs Siddons, warning them not to infringe upon her rights as holder of the Royal Patent. This received the somewhat snooty reply that, while the Ryders were ignorant of what the rights of Mrs Siddons were, they could not be greater than the exclusive rights of Drury Lane and Covent Garden and, since there were a number of minor theatres in London, surely there could be at least one in Edinburgh.

In other words, the Ryders were prepared to defy openly the Theatre Royal monopoly. After a lengthy correspondence—in which every attempt was made to make the Ryders see reason—Harriet Siddons applied for an interdict, which took some time to be granted. The case finally came to court on 24 February, 1825.

The Ryders put up a spirited defence on a number of specious grounds, including one which involved the telling of a quite bare-faced lie. The plays presented at the Caledonian, it was claimed, fell outwith the scope of the Theatres Act, in that they were not true 'entertainments of the stage' and, as such, required no licence from the Lord Chamberlain. This, of course, was a similar defence to that which Natali Corri had successfully used in 1812—but, on this occasion, it simply would not hold water. While it was true that Shakespeare's

Mrs Harriet Siddons: after the portrait by Robert Smirke
Courtesy of the McManus Galleries, Dundee

plays had been altered for this purpose by means of changing the title—*Richard III*, for instance, became *The Battle of Bosworth Field*—and adding music to the poetry, this was certainly not the general rule at the Caledonian. It seems incredible that Ryder had the nerve to make such a claim when he had been playing *Rob Roy* all winter!

For this and other reasons—concerning complicated points of law—the case was lost and a fine of £50 imposed on the Ryders. In addition to this, an interdict was granted to Mrs Siddons but, as Dibdin remarks in *The Annals of the Edinburgh Stage*, 'no better commentary on the value of that dread sentence can be given than the fact that Ryder went on playing just the same in spite of it!' The Ryders continued in Edinburgh for two more seasons, finally leaving the Caledonian in the spring of 1827. This must have been particularly galling to Harriet Siddons, who had gone to a great deal of trouble and expense to bring the case to court.

As far as her brother was concerned, it is difficult to know what William Murray thought of it all. He could not, however, have felt much concern. This was the period at which the Theatre Royal was at the very height of its prosperity, a fact which played no small part in the demise of Henry Johnston's initiative at the Caledonian. Murray probably reasoned that, if he could see off the competition of the most popular actor in Scotland, he need not be too concerned about Corbet Ryder. At the very least, he must have known that, in any struggle between the theatres, the Theatre Royal had all the advantage.

Shortly after the court case, the Ryders, in what must be seen as a retaliatory move, halved the prices at the Caledonian. In response to this, Murray simply followed suit and cut the Theatre Royal prices. Although this delighted the Ryders, who lost no time in announcing the 'Proud Triumph of the Caledonian in compelling the Theatre Royal to follow its example', the fact remains that, while Murray could well afford this loss of revenue, the Ryders could not. Nor could they afford to incur the hostility of the theatrical press.

As mentioned in Chapter 3, there was a profusion of theatre journals in Edinburgh at this time. Most of these were written under pseudonyms, by men who were lawyers by profession and who, naturally enough, did not take kindly to the open defiance of an interdict. Several attacks on the Ryder company appeared in print, the most malicious of which appeared in the *Edinburgh Dramatic Recorder* of March, 1825.

While purporting to be an objective review of the talents of the Ryder company, this piece is full of barbs which deliberately undercut anything positive that is said about the performers. Corbet Ryder himself, for instance, is described as follows.

> In the pursuit of his avocations, we believe he has acquired a considerable sum of money; and the successful result of his recent bold speculation must have added very considerably to his former gains. As an actor, we think much less of him—and the only thing, indeed, that we have ever seen him do in a passable manner is Rob Roy. He looks the character to admiration—but he can neither act nor speak it. His voice sings in his throat—his lips catch the words, and clip and curtail them of their fair proportions, while they endeavour to escape from his mouth. His action is unvaried, stiff and formal. In all limited companies, however, Mr Ryder must take parts which his better sense should tell him he is unfit for...

Most of the other actors fared no better. The Irish actor Paddy Weekes, for instance, a long-serving member of the Ryder company and one of its most enduring assets, was rated

> much lower than any other performer...he can neither embody—although he may embowel—the character he represents, nor give utterance to a line without some fright-ful gag—which will not make even a single barren spectator laugh.

One actor was described as being 'easily frightened', while another apparently walked 'as if his shoes were filled with unboiled pease'. Even the ladies of the company did not escape censure. Miss Pindar 'has a tolerable share of pantomimic ability; exhibits, as often as she can, a pair of well-shaped legs'. Miss Edmiston is praised for her graceful figure 'though her bust is by no means full and her face is deficient of expression'. The Ryder twins, who could not have been much older than twelve at the time, had 'all the hobble-de-thump accompaniments so essential to the vulgarities of antiquated capering'. The most vicious cut of all, however, was directed at their mother.

> We remember—with no ungrateful feelings—the impression she first made upon us many years ago in Aberdeen, when, as the blushing Juliet, she breathed her first and virgin vow of innocent love to the passionate Romeo of her husband...she has now left the stage to younger, if not better, aspirants and has betaken herself to the more weighty, if not more laudable, employment of looking after the receipts. And yet we should like to see the old lady—and she must be an old lady now—once more. Certes, the first time we see her name on the bills, our presence shall not be wanting at the Caledonian.

At the time that the above words were written, Jessie Ryder was just 27 years of age!

In the face of such hostility, it is hardly surprising that the Ryders were eventually forced out of Edinburgh. Their lease was taken over in 1827 by Charles Bass, who had been playing the Northern Circuit in their absence from his base in Dundee. It is indicative of the animosity that existed between the Ryders and the Theatre Royal—or rather, one suspects, between Jessie and Harriet—that Bass ran the Caledonian for several years without any difficulty from his competition.

As for the Ryders, they returned to the pattern of production they had followed in the days before their Edinburgh venture: winter seasons in Aberdeen, followed by tours on the Northern Circuit. In 1829, family involvement in the company was extended when Corbet's son, Tom, made his debut. Unlike his father, Tom was not a leading man but a comedian in the style of Mackay. He was also a very capable manager and, before too long, took over the running of the company, allowing his parents to concentrate on their acting.

Under Tom's management, the Circuit was extended to include the towns of Forfar, Stonehaven, Inverness and many smaller places. There is evidence to suggest that these visits were generally well received. In a an article which appeared in the *Era Almanac* of 1868 Andrew Halliday (a playwright who was best known for his adaptations of Scott and Dickens) recalled the regular visits of the Ryder company to the town of Banff.

> The gentry and the well-to-do people of the town bought tickets and distributed them among their servants and the poor children of the town. An eccentric country Laird brought all his people down in a cart when his favourite play was performed. When the pathetic passages were being delivered, Sir John used to turn round to the girls in the back benches and urge them to weep. 'Greet, queans, greet' Sir John used to say, and the girls immediately plunged their faces into their pocket handkerchiefs and appeared to be deeply afffected. Sir John also led the applause, and shook his fist and frowned when the back benches failed to take up the points.

Just how regular these tours were is rather difficult to say; existing records suggest that they were sporadic but, since most information comes from collections of surviving playbills—which are, almost by definition, incomplete—activity might have been greater than they suggest. The fact is, however, that the Ryder company, under Tom's management, maintained a presence on the Circuit for the next 30 years.

Towards the end of the first decade, however, two significant changes took place. The first of these occurred in 1839, with the death of Corbet Ryder. This not only robbed the family of its father but the company of its leading man and most important asset. The saying among Scottish theatre managers in those days was 'when in doubt, play *Rob Roy*' and Corbet had been the most celebrated Rob of his time. He was replaced in the company for some years by Thomas Langley, an actor who had been running short seasons at Dundee.

The death of Corbet had another effect, however. The evenly-balanced play policy which, as we have seen, had contributed to the company's initial success, was faithfully maintained during Corbet's lifetime. After his death, this balance was disturbed by a greater emphasis on National Drama, in which medium Tom's talents as a comedian could be seen to greater advantage. It should not be supposed that this was done for reasons of vanity; the simple fact was that, with Corbet gone, Tom had become the company's major attraction.

In 1843, the stage was transformed by the repeal of Walpole's Theatres Act. This measure, for which actors and playwrights had been campaigning for more than a decade, changed the face of theatre in Scotland completely. It introduced an era of free trade, in which the kind of competition that the Ryders had attempted in Edinburgh 20 years earlier was now conducted on a more equitable basis. In the same year that this came into effect, Jessie Ryder met and married a young actor called John Pollock. Of this match, Frank Boyd remarks, rather unkindly, in his *Records of the Dundee Stage* that 'when Jessie Fraser married Corbet Ryder, she was many years his junior; in her second marriage, the opposite was true'. Despite the difference in their ages, however, Jessie outlived her second husband by almost 20 years!

As for Tom Ryder, he seems to have managed a completely different company and toured the Circuit, more or less successfully, from 1843 on. In his personal life, Tom had a tendency to indulge his weaknesses and his extravagance was notorious. 'Corbet Ryder's wastrel son' wrote local historian J M Bulloch many years later, 'died like a beggar as he had lived like a prince'. Even so, he never lost his popularity. Just as he had replaced his father with Langley—and, later, with the Irish actor, G V Brooke—he found, in Julia Nicol, a more than adequate replacement for his mother.

Tom continued to travel the Circuit until his death in 1872, which took place in unhappy circumstances. Apart from the fact that he was severely troubled by gout, he was found guilty in a rather squalid defamation case, involving a country laird and one of the actresses in his company. Tom, apparently, had fallen in love with this young woman, who had turned him down for the young laird. Out of jealousy, Tom had published some malicious rumours about his younger rival and had paid the penalty. It was said that he died from the scandal as much as from the gout.

After her marriage to Pollock, Jessie concentrated her energies almost exclusively on the Aberdeen Theatre Royal, although she would frequently appear with Tom's company if she was required. As for Pollock, he seems to have been the junior partner in every sense, the only mention of him in the records—apart from his acting—being a singularly dramatic one, involving the Irish actor, Barry Sullivan. Sullivan, the company's leading man at the time, was playing a love scene with Jessie so convincingly that it gave her husband considerable offence. Pollock promptly strode on stage and, in full view of the audience, knocked Sullivan down!

It is not recorded what Jessie thought of this rather unusual management decision, but it is likely that she was far from amused. According to all reports, she was somewhat dictatorial in her management style, carrying out her business with great spirit and energy. J Keith Angus in his *A Scotch Play-house* (Aberdeen, 1878) gives us the following description of her management.

> Her great stage experience, not to speak of natural abilities, rendered her an admirable manageress. She had a quick and generally accurate appreciation of talent in young beginners, and though the training in her school was a severe one, it produced all the better fruit for that; and we shall be quite within the mark in saying that hundreds in the theatrical profession could speak gratefully of the days they spent under her tuition.

One of the first of her pupils was a young Edinburgh girl called Agnes Robertson who, together with her husband Dion Boucicault, would take America by storm in the 1850s. One of the last was a young actor from Yorkshire whose name would become familiar to Scottish play-goers a century later, when his grandson ran a successful repertory company in Edinburgh, Glasgow and Aberdeen: Wilson Barrett.

By the time that Barrett came along, however, Jessie Pollock had all but given up management in favour of her son-in-law, A D McNeill. An Edinburgh man, McNeill had nevertheless started his career in London, where he had spent two years at the Lyceum, then under the management of Charles Dillon. After a few years in Birmingham (where he became a popular favourite in leading rôles), he returned to Scotland and joined the company at Aberdeen. He married one of the Ryder twins, Jessie, in 1852 and took over the management in 1862. (Emma, the other twin, also married a member of the company, Edward Price, who later took over from McNeill.)

Even after she had retired from management, however, Jessie continued to work as an actress and, in fact, did not retire completely from the stage until 1869, when she was 72 years of age. Her vitality and youthfulness of spirit is amply illustrated by the fact that she was still playing Lucy Ashton in *The Bride of Lammermoor* when she was over 50 years old!

For all that she owed to the Scott dramas, however, her own personal favourites were Shakespeare, Sheridan and Goldsmith. According to her obituarist in the *Aberdeen Free Press*, she would often aver that these playwrights could not be matched for 'scene, invention, elegance of dialogue or spontaneity of humour'. In her youth, she had played Lady Macbeth opposite the great Macready and it was in this favourite—some would say appropriate—character that Robert Innes, the portrait painter, depicted her at the time of her final retirement in 1869. This painting, the cost of which was raised by public subscription, hung for many years in the foyer of Her Majesty's Theatre, Aberdeen. The fact that Mrs Pollock's portrait now seems to have vanished from the face of the earth is a measure of the transience of the performer's art—not to mention the philistinism which, all too often, prevails in Scottish society.

Jessie Fraser/Ryder/Pollock was certainly no philistine. On the contrary, she devoted the greater part of her life to the promotion of her art, not only in her native city but throughout Scotland. Together with her first husband and her step-son, she pioneered the tradition of touring productions that is still such a notable feature of Scottish theatrical life today. To a greater extent than any other Scottish actress, she helped to create the theatre of her time.

Allardice Nicoll, in his *History of the English Drama 1660-1900* (Cambridge, 1955), has the following to say about the first half of the nineteenth century.

> There is something which tells us that a passage over the year 1800 will carry us at once into the midst of an epoch which seems to be, or at least gives the foundation for, that which we call modern. Definite links, some literary, some historic, some by personal relations easily carry the mind back to this half-century and the mental picture has a certain nearness that is lacking in the more artificial revisualisations of August or Caroline times.

Jessie Pollock's career coincided with this period more or less exactly. Although, towards the end of her life, she would often deplore the changes that were taking place in the theatre, there is little doubt of the contribution that she herself made to such changes. In her time, she saw the theatre shrug off the lowly and slightly disreputable status of the eighteenth century to emerge as a notable feature of Scottish urban life.

It is something of an irony, therefore, to note that this transformation in the theatre's fortunes was seen at its most dramatic in a part of Scotland that Mrs Pollock visited only on rare occasions—the great city of Glasgow.

Chapter Six

THE GLASGOW BOYS

The Glasgow Theatre has a history that is completely different from that of Edinburgh. Lacking the status of national capital, there was no pressure to invite comparison with London, and Glasgow never had its own equivalent of the Elibank Group. Nor did Glasgow people ever express any interest in learning 'the English language'; elecution was certainly taught in the city, but much later than in Edinburgh and never for such a political purpose. At least until the formation of the Glasgow Repertory Company in 1909, theatre in Glasgow developed along similar lines to most other British provincial centres.

In pre-Industrial times, Glasgow was a smaller and altogether more attractive city than it is today. Daniel Defoe once described it as the most beautiful little town in Great Britain, an opinion that was shared by others, including Tobias Smollet and Dorothy Wordsworth. At this time, however, it was also a very Presbyterian town, a place where the ministers wielded even more influence than they did in Edinburgh. The Glasgow Presbytery, moreover, was not only stricter in belief—being mostly of the so-called Evangelical Party in the Church— but was considerably less respectful of lawful authority. (Interestingly enough, none of the Glasgow ministers seemed to be aware of the provisions of the Theatres Act and the whole question of legality never seems to have been taken up.) Early attempts to establish a theatre in Glasgow had been frustrated, not by recourse to the law as in Edinburgh, but by physical violence.

The experience of Glasgow's first working theatre is a typical example. This was in Alston Street, close to the site of the present Central Station, and was built in 1764 by a group of Glasgow merchants, headed by James Dunlop of Garnkirk, who employed David Beat of the Canongate Theatre in Edinburgh as manager. On the very night of its opening, a fanatical mob, egged on by a preacher, entered the theatre and set it on fire. Fortunately, the structural damage was slight and the theatre was repaired and re-opened. It was managed by Beat—who appears to have been undismayed by the experience of the Stayley riot in 1767—

and a succession of others, with little real success, until 1782, when it was burned down again—this time by accident. Just before this mishap occurred, the owners took a new partner—the ubiquitous John Jackson, who had recently purchased the Theatre Royal in Edinburgh.

When his partners considered re-building the fire-damaged theatre, Jackson suggested that another site be chosen, since he felt that Alston Street was not central enough. Accordingly, a new theatre was built at St Enoch's Croft, now known as Dunlop Street—and it was in this house, the Caledonian, that the fortunes of theatre in Glasgow were turned around. The Caledonian became the most successful Glasgow theatre of its time and remained in business for most of the next century. As for Jackson, Glasgow presented him with the most successful—and certainly the happiest—management of his career.

Jackson's character is perhaps best exemplified by the attitude he took to the Stayley Riot, which he witnessed at first hand, being a member of the audience on that evening. In his memoirs—the audaciously mis-named *A History of the Scottish Stage*—he makes it plain that he had little use for Stayley, either as an actor or as a man. However, he does admit that, had the management of the Canongate Theatre been in his hands, Stayley would have been engaged and much trouble and expense avoided. It was this kind of pragmatism that made Jackson an effective manager.

Jackson's readiness to stand firm in the face of any opposition is possibly the most attractive aspect of his character. This was a quality which was to stand him in good stead in Glasgow. Very shortly after the Caledonian opened for business, heavy rainfall caused the Clyde to break its banks and Glasgow experienced one of the worst floods in its history, during which a great many people lost their homes. Jackson's strenuous efforts to aid the dispossessed—by using his theatre to raise funds etc.—made him many friends in the city. His new-found popularity inevitably led to an increase of business.

Jackson's first period of management lasted for almost ten years—until his bankruptcy in 1791—during which time he managed his Edinburgh and Glasgow theatres simultaneously. If this seems difficult to understand, it should be remembered that, at this time, the Edinburgh audience could only support three playing nights during the season, while the Glasgow house could barely manage two. By co-ordinating his programme to accommodate both theatres, Jackson was able to make the most of his resources. This approach was successful enough to bear repetition—in one form or another—by various managements over the next two hundred years.

It was under Jackson, too, that the stock company system became established in Scotland. Since the main thrust of Jackson's policy relied heavily on the engagement of London stars, he had to ensure that his company was composed of actors who could, as nearly as was possible, replicate the support these stars had received in London. This meant, in effect, employing mostly English actors who, for one reason or another, had been unable to find a place in London.

In short, Jackson's methods were those of a successful English provincial manager of the time. Although, for reasons that have already been given, they made no impression whatsoever in Edinburgh, they worked well enough in Glasgow and his other theatres. Even so, it has to be recognised that such methods are always ultimately self-defeating. A theatre must be something more than simply a place where one can view famous visitors. Irrespective of his personal popularity, therefore, neither Jackson or his theatre ever succeeded in becoming an integral part of the Glasgow community.

Jackson's bankruptcy ended the first and most fruitful period of his Glasgow management. It would be another nine years before his affairs would be sufficiently organised for him to return. By this time, however, he was a shadow of his former self. Shortly before his death in 1806, the *Monthly Mirror* made the following assessment of his management.

> The experience of this and the two or three last seasons ought to convince Mr John Jackson that the tide of popularity, while never in his favour, has irretrievably turned against him. It would be 'kicking against the pricks' to attempt a new management.

It soon became evident, however, that the blame for the Caledonian's decline could not be laid completely at Jackson's door. It was at this time that the size and character of Glasgow began to change, and it experienced a growth in population which would continue unabated for the rest of the century. One early manifestation of this change was the founding of the Queen Street Theatre Royal, a theatrical competitor which was virtually unbeatable. This being the case, Jackson's successors—including Charles Kemble, Macready Senior and even, for a short time, William Murray—fared little better. The Caledonian began to decline rapidly and, by 1823, an anonymous Glasgow theatre-goer was moved to write to the *Edinburgh Dramatic Review*, describing the company as 'a most paltry and insignicant set' and the manager as follows.

> I have observed in one of your Numbers, in criticizing the performance of *Rob Roy*, that you are rather severe on the acting of Mr Calcraft in the hero of the piece; but, sir, you may be happy that you have not such a representative of it as we have. It has lately been performed here by a Mr Seymour, who has no qualification for the character. With him it is all rant from beginning to end; and in those parts where he ought to be pathetic, he is noisy in the extreme. His action is more fitted for a porter in the Broomielaw than a performer on the stage...

Perhaps, however, the letter was not as anonymous as it seems—for this attack on Seymour, hints at a very particular indentity. In the same year in which the letter was written, 1823, effective theatre—in every possible sense of that word— arrived at Dunlop Street in the person of John Henry Alexander.

Alexander, born in Dunbar in 1792, was one of the few Scottish managers of the time who was actually Scottish by birth. As a boy, he had apparently determined on an acting career after seeing Harry Johnston play *Douglas*. His first engagement was at Dumfries in 1814, where he was a member of the local

John Henry Alexander
Courtesy of the People's Palace, Glasgow

company supporting Dorothy Jordan in that season. In 1815, he joined Murray's company at the Edinburgh Theatre Royal as a utility player but very quickly established himself in leading rôles. He played Rashleigh Osbaldistone in the famous 1819 production of *Rob Roy* and his other parts included Dandie Dinmont in *Guy Mannering*, and Jamie Ratcliffe in *The Heart of Midlothian*. Although he had obviously become a valued member of Murray's company, it was at this time that his somewhat odd, egocentric behaviour began to manifest itself.

In 1820, Alexander was appointed manager of the theatre in Carlisle. Since this theatre operated under the statute of 1788, it had a very short summer season and this engagement need not have conflicted with his obligations in Edinburgh. In spite of this, however, Alexander felt that his new position entitled him to an increase in salary and he wrote to Murray, asking for another ten shillings a week. Murray refused and there was a prolonged argument between the two men, culminating in an acrimonious confrontation which took place—in a manner that Alexander would make uniquely his own—during a performance on the stage of the Theatre Royal. Murray was absolutely furious about this and, as punishment, refused to allow Alexander to take his benefit. Nothing daunted, Alexander hired the Leith Walk theatre for one night and, after a profitable performance there, set out for Carlisle to begin his managerial career.

After three years in Carlisle, during which he also managed the autumn season in Dumfries, Alexander turned his attention to Glasgow. The aim of his managerial strategy was quite plain: to establish a circuit based in Glasgow and taking in the southern theatres. Initially, however, he was to be disappointed. When he applied for the lease of the Caledonian, he found he had been forestalled by Frank Seymour, at that time stage-manager at the Queen Street Theatre Royal. It was at this time that the above attack on Seymour was made in the *Edinburgh Dramatic Review*.

The fact is that Alexander was unwilling to concede defeat. On discovering that Seymour's lease did not cover the whole building and that a large cellar—formerly occupied by a potato merchant—remained vacant, he decided to set up in competition. He obtained the lease of the cellar, fitted it up as a theatre and named it the Dominion of Fancy. This led to one of the most farcical episodes in the entire history of the stage.

Seymour opened at the Caledonian with a production of *Macbeth*. On the same night, Alexander opened the Dominion of Fancy with a spectacular melodrama entitled *The Battle of Inch*. Walter Baynham, in his *History of the Glasgow Stage*, describes the result.

> Macbeth was acted nearly throughout to the tuneful accompaniment of the shouts of the soldiery, the clanging of dish covers, the clashing of swords, the banging of drums, with the fumes of blue fire every now and then rising through the chinks of the planks from the stage below to the stage above. The audience laughed and this stimulated the wrath of the combative managers.

It was not long before retaliation followed from Seymour, who employed a brass band upstairs to drown out Alexander's performances. Alexander lodged a complaint with the Court of Session, which led to an attempt at compromise; Alexander was to be allowed the two best playing nights, Friday and Saturday, on condition that he let Seymour have a free hand for the rest of the week. The spirit of compromise, however, was always alien to Alexander's nature and, before long, both managers were back in court, Seymour complaining that his rival had broken the agreement. Clearly impatient with the situation, the magistrates ruled that 'neither party was to annoy the other and, on any more complaints being brought, both places would be ordered to be closed'.

This stopped the litigation but not the conflict. Seymour lifted the planking of the Caledonian floor and poured water down on Alexander's performance. Alexander retaliated by duplicating Seymour's programme, staging the same plays simultaneously. Matters came to a head during a production of *Die Frieschutz*, when Seymour's supporters succeeded in reducing Alexander's performance to chaos. Undeterred, however, Alexander persisted with his skirmishing and the battle continued for as long as Seymour remained at the Caledonian.

One would have thought that these events would be extremely destructive of business but the opposite, in fact, was the case. The public flocked in their droves to witness such antics. In 1828, for instance, a performance of *Tom and Jerry* ran for a month at both houses—an enormous run in Glasgow at that time. The rival theatres became so popular, in fact, that the Queen Street Theatre Royal soon found itself in difficulties. These proved to be serious enough for the manager to decide to solve his problems by simply disappearing, leaving a stack of debts behind. Seymour was appointed in his place, leaving the field clear for Alexander to take over at the Caledonian. That was the end of the Dominion of Fancy.

Alexander remained in control of the theatre for the rest of his life. As for his rival, Seymour enjoyed some success at Queen Street—mainly by engaging such attractions as the renowned horseman Andrew Ducrow and the great comedian John Liston—but his career was brought to an untimely end when the Queen Street house was destroyed by fire in 1829. The Patent was put up for auction and Alexander was the successful bidder. From then on, the Caledonian was known as the Theatre Royal, Glasgow.

Dibdin, in his *Annals of the Edinburgh Stage*, tells us that Alexander's management 'it may be safely said, did almost as much for the drama in the West as Murray did for it in the East'. This, however, is to take an extremely charitable view. While it is true that Alexander had a large measure of succes at Dunlop Street, this was achieved through his eccentricity rather than any considered policy. It is also true that he sought to imitate Murray—his former employer and, at that time, the leading figure on the Scottish stage—but he did so in a manner that produced a grotesque parody of the Edinburgh manager's methods.

For instance, in Chapter 3, it was mentioned that Murray was jealous of his position as Patent-holder and would challenge any interloper through the courts—but this only applied to genuine competition. Murray would never have dreamed of acting against the penny gaffs and acting booths that had begun to spring up in the Old Town at that time. Alexander, on the other hand, loved litigation and prowled around Glasgow looking for people to sue. Until the repeal of the Theatres Act in 1843, Alexander was successful in closing down every competitor, great and small, who threatened his position. His victims included genuine rivals like David Miller, who later opened the Adelphi on Glasgow Green, and John Henry Anderson, the so-called 'Wizard of the North' whose sumptuous but short-lived City Theatre—it had a capacity of 4,000 and a working life of just ten weeks—later became a focus of discontent. At the other extreme, he also succeeded in obtaining an interdict against a man called Pindar, a man who organised shows in a booth whose daytime use was that of a barber-shop. On one occasion, he even brought an successful action against Mumford, an Englishman who ran a disorderly—although very popular—play-booth in the Saltmarket.

In his production methods, too, Alexander sought to emulate Murray and imposed a rigid discipline in directing his performers. There was a major difference, though. Whereas Murray restricted his direction to rehearsal, Alexander often carried his into performance!

The whole time Mr Alexander was on the stage, he was directing everybody, players, scene-shifters and gas-men, saying, for instance, audibly 'Come down here, sir.' 'Stand

you there, sir.' 'MacStuart, that's not your place.' 'Keep time with the air as I do.'
'Hold up your head, sir.' He beat time to the orchestra; he spoke to the musicians; he
sang the music for other people and he spoke their words.

That description of Alexander's onstage behaviour appeared in the *Glasgow
Dramatic Review*, a journal which was always hostile to his management, as
indeed most publications appeared to be. There was more to these attacks, however, than personal animosity.

During the course of Alexander's management, Glasgow underwent a meta-
morphosis from small academic town to large industrial conurbation. In 1823,
when Alexander began, the population had been 147,000; 30 years later, it had
grown to 359,000 and was rising rapidly. With this increase in size came a change
in character and one important manifestation was the great divide that sprang up
between rich and poor. For better or worse, theatre began to be perceived as a
pastime of the privileged class. This perception which, as we have seen, was
triumphantly defeated by Murray in Edinburgh, had begun to take root in Glasgow and would, in the future, lead to a certain perverse strain of artistic snob-
bery which would become increasingly noticeable in the theatrical affairs of
Glasgow and which would do considerable damage in the years that lay ahead.
At the time, however, this attitude was reflected in the persistent hostility towards Alexander that appeared in the Glasgow press.

This hostility did not seem to trouble Alexander one bit—in fact, he appeared
to relish it. Taking the attitude that no publicity is bad publicity, he frequently
retaliated to press criticism in the correspondence columns of Glasgow newspapers, often stirring up controversy where none existed. In 1843, for instance,
one such 'paper battle' broke out over some observations that were printed in
the *Glasgow Argus*.

The background to this correspondence is fairly simple. In the summer of
1843, a company from the Theatre Royal, Edinburgh, visited Dunlop Street to
play a short season of just seven nights. Such visits, it should be said, were fairly
common at this time; the relationship between the Edinburgh and Glasgow theatres was a good one and Alexander would often bring a company from the Glasgow Theatre Royal to Edinburgh for a similar visit. On this occasion, however,
the management was not in the hands of Murray but of H F Lloyd. By this time,
Lloyd was well settled in Scotland and ambitious to try his hand at management.
Wishing, no doubt, to encourage his assistant, Murray agreed to appear in Glasgow under Lloyd's management. The season proved a great success, so much so
that Lloyd asked Alexander for an extension of two more nights. This was refused on the grounds that the theatre had been let to another party. Since Lloyd
knew of no other party, he was a little puzzled by this but, of course, had no
choice but to accept Alexander's decision. His company took their final bow
and returned to Edinburgh—and that should have been the end of the matter.

When it transpired, however, that this 'other party' was non-existent and
that the theatre had remained dark for the two nights in question, the *Argus*
published a report in which it was suggested that Alexander had acted out of

pique, being jealous of the Edinburgh company's success. Alexander responded to this with a very long letter in the *Glasgow Herald* in which he abused Lloyd for a 'gross want of courtesy' for placing himself and his family on the free list. Lloyd, having paid rent for the theatre, regarded himself as being in possession for the duration of the season but, with intended courtesy, had arranged for Alexander and his family to be admitted without payment. This, to Alexander's mind, carried the suggestion that he must seek permission to enter his own theatre and was his true reason for refusing to grant the extension. Matters were only made worse when Lloyd wrote to set matters straight.

Alexander's reply was even more abusive. Describing the Edinburgh manager as the 'successful hero of seven nights', he further suggested that 'little Sancho Panza is not himself alone', implying that Murray had been behind the whole business. In the course of this intemperate correspondence, however, Alexander lost no opportunity of reminding the Glasgow public at large of the achievement of his own management.

The achievement was very considerable indeed. Although Alexander never enjoyed the prestige or reputation of William Murray, he certainly matched the Edinburgh manager in the business he created. By 1840, Alexander had become the sole proprietor of Dunlop Street, enabling him to carry out major alterations which would make the Glasgow Theatre Royal, with a capacity of almost 3,000 seats, the largest theatre in Scotland. During the course of Alexander's management—which was to last for more than 20 years— he was never in financial difficulty, for the simple reason that he never lost his popularity with the Glasgow audience. Journalists might have deplored his eccentricities—his habit in performance, for instance, of coming out of character in order to threaten some heckler with eviction—but Glasgow people loved these departures from theatrical convention and, in fact, flocked to Dunlop Street just to see Alexander in action.

If, however, Alexander's management had begun with comedy—not to say farce—it was to end in tragedy. On the evening of Saturday, 17 February, 1849, the Dunlop Street Theatre Royal was to be the scene of the greatest calamity ever to take place in any Scottish theatre.

The theatre was full to capacity that night, a large proportion of the audience being young men and women who had come to see the pantomime. This was preceded by a military melodrama entitled *The Siege of Calais*, in which Alexander was playing the leading part. The manager was therefore on the stage and in costume at the moment when the disastrous events of the evening began to unfold.

At between seven and eight o'clock, just after the first act of the melodrama had come down, somebody shouted 'Fire!' Now, fire was always a very great danger in Victorian theatres—which were mostly made of wood—but the fear was particularly acute in Glasgow at that time. The above-mentioned City Theatre had been destroyed by fire just ten weeks after its opening four years earlier, and two recent fires had destroyed other theatres: Miller's Adelphi and Cooke's

Circus. Understandably, therefore, the cry sent a frisson of fear through the audience.

As it happened, the alarm proved to be false. One of the gas jets had malfunctioned, creating some sparks and a little smoke. Some of the theatre staff—including one James Finlay, who apparently doused what little fire there was with his cloth cap—attended to the problem and soon had matters under control. The audience cheered, the band struck up and everyone settled down to watch the show. Unfortunately, after the initial alarm, someone had thought to call the Fire Brigade. The sight of fire-helmets in the auditorium—suggesting that the fire had not, after all, been extinguished—prompted a general panic and there was a headlong rush for the main staircase that led to the street. In a very short time, 800 people found themselves trapped on that staircase, ensuring that the rush quickly became a crush in which scores of lives were lost.

The part Alexander played in this disaster was a truly heroic one. Together with two of his actors, Langley and Younge, he toiled all night to rescue as many as he could from the melee—on more than one occasion, risking his own safety—and saw to it that the wounded received attention. The Garrick Hotel, across the road, was pressed into service as a temporary hospital and many private citizens in the neighbourhood opened their doors to the wounded. Despite all efforts, however, by the morning the death-toll had reached 70, mostly teenage boys who had been out with their girls for the evening. Only six of the dead were female, including the most poignant case of all: a little girl of just three years of age.

After that night, Alexander was never the same again. Two years later, in 1851, he signed over his management to a Mr Simpson of Birmingham and before that year had ended, broken in spirit, he passed away. He was to be greatly missed, for despite his quarrelsome manner, his love of controversy and his almost legendary meanness, he was known to be a man of rigid honesty who devoted his every waking moment to the service of the Glasgow public. Apart from that, John Henry Alexander—or 'Alick' as he was always affectionately known—was a true character who enjoyed a great deal of esteem in a city where such characters have always been cherished.

Mr Simpson of Birmingham does not appear to have remained in Glasgow for very long, for in 1852, Dunlop Street came into the hands of a very different actor, albeit one who, like Alexander, had been a regular member of Murray's company at the Edinburgh Theatre Royal. Edmund Glover was born in 1813 to a theatrical family, being the eldest son of Julia Glover, whose long career earned her the title of 'the mother of the stage'. He began by playing small rôles at the Haymarket where Murray, on one of his frequent trips to London, spotted him and issued an invitation to join the Edinburgh company. Although he had been engaged to play 'leading business', Glover made his Edinburgh debut in 1841 in a somewhat curious rôle. For some reason, Murray decided to introduce his new leading man to Edinburgh audiences by casting him as a Highland outlaw, Donacha Dhu in *The Whistler of the Glen*, a new—and as it turned out unsuccessful—

attempt to stage the hitherto undramatised third volume of *The Heart of Midlothian*. Since Glover was a Londoner through and through, it must surely have been a baptism of fire!

He soon proved his worth as an accomplished and versatile performer—not only an actor, but a dancer, a pantomimist, an able swordsman and a more than competent painter. Over the next six years, Glover was a regular member of Murray's company, playing mostly classical leading rôles: Othello, Macbeth, Richard III, Shylock and Creon in *Antigone*. He also appears to have been a very fine Rob Roy, as the following account by Walter Baynham testifies.

> It was of a more homely type, abounding in strangely effective traits; never failing in his impersonation of the 'bold outlaw' to give glimpses here and there that Rob was a man strongly attached to wife, weans, clan and dear old Scotland.

Among the many talents that Glover possessed was an acute business instinct. On a visit to London in 1847, he went to a concert to hear the Swedish soprano, Jenny Lind. He was so impressed that he immediately arranged to meet the singer and engaged her to sing in a series of concerts in Edinburgh, Glasgow and Perth. It was the profit he made in this enterprise—some £3,000—that persuaded Glover to go into management. He decided on Glasgow rather than Edinburgh and took a large hall in West Nile Street, which he re-named the Prince's Theatre.

Almost the first action that Glover took on entering his Glasgow management was to invite H F Lloyd to join him. Lloyd had no trouble in accepting and at once wrote to Murray for his release. This was immediately granted, but when Lloyd tried to push his luck and asked for a benefit before leaving, Murray refused. Like Alexander before him, Lloyd hired another venue—in this case the Music Hall—and enjoyed a profitable evening in Edinburgh before joining Glover in Glasgow. He was to return three years later when, on Murray's retirement, he took over the management of the Theatre Royal. As it happens, this coincided with Glover's accession at Dunlop Street.

Edmund Glover always believed that Glasgow was potentially, as he put it, a 'good theatrical city'—and it was in Glasgow that he was to make his mark. Although his management was of a comparatively short duration, the popularity he enjoyed in the city was so great that, even today, the name of Glover remains associated with Glasgow theatre. His intentions were clear from the outset: he would model his Glasgow management on the methods and style of the Edinburgh Theatre Royal, mounting the same plays in the same style, using many of the same actors that Murray employed—although some of them were, naturally enough, more popular in Glasgow than they had been in Edinburgh and vice versa. (*Guy Mannering*, for instance, was always the most popular Waverley drama as far as Glasgow was concerned, with *Rob Roy* only making occasional appearances.) Like Murray, too, he began and ended each season with an address to the audience. The following, which is an extract from his first address, gives some impression of Glover's informal, rather likeable style.

> Ladies and Gentlemen—Here we are in Dunlop Street! I feel so nervous and excited tonight that I am sure you will pardon me, and not attribute to any want of proper respect my somewhat limited address to you; and for eloquence of tongue accept the silent (but more genuine) eloquence of the heart. I feel to stand, as I do, in the presence of you, the enlightened citizens of this great community, on the stage of this splendid theatre, lessee and director...it is one of the proudest events of my life. My past career has, I trust, shown my earnest desire to uphold the character of the profession; and the future, I hope, shall prove the sincerity of my intention. If I act well as manager, will you not support me as public? You will—I feel assured you will—and if you do not, I believe the blame will be my own—without your help, I can do nothing. With it, everything.

This adoption of Murray's methods was not simply a sedulous imitation of the Edinburgh manager but an indication of how much Glover had learned from the experience of working with him. He did not follow Murray's practices slavishly however and, in one respect at least, the practice of the Glasgow manager differed sharply from that of his Edinburgh mentor. As Glover's Glasgow management prospered, he began to build a circuit; he took out leases at Paisley and Dunfermline and, in 1859, he opened a new theatre in Greenock. He never quite severed his connection with Edinburgh, though, and continued to visit the capital to play leading rôles for the rest of his life.

As mentioned above, this is also true of the actors in his company, most of whom have been dealt with in an earlier context. There was, however, one actor who figured largely in Glover's plans and who—though no stranger to Edinburgh—became something of a fixture at Dunlop Street. Glover's close associate—eventual son-in-law and intended successor—was Tom Powrie, regarded by many at that time as the greatest Scottish actor who ever lived.

Powrie, who was born in Dundee in 1824, began acting at a very early age. The story is told that, when he was a schoolboy at Stirling's School in Dundee's Tay Street, he fitted up a stable there and organised a company of his peers to present a melodrama called *Macglashan* to an audience of other children, the charge for admission being three pins per head! As he grew up, he continued to develop his acting skills as an amateur until, in 1843 at the age of 19, he made his professional debut as a member of the stock company at Dundee's Yeaman Shore theatre, his first part being that of Roderick Dhu in an adaptation of Scott's *The Lady of the Lake*. He remained in Dundee for several seasons under the management of Langley—the same Langley who assisted Alexander during the fire panic of 1849—until he joined Glover's company, who were playing a short engagement at Newcastle, in 1848. On his debut in Glasgow in 1849, the *North British Mail* carried the following notice.

> The character of Shylock is a most trying one for a young actor; the Jew is stricken in years and his bosom is torn with conflicting passions; his hatred of Christians, his revenge against Antonio, and the pertinacity in which he sticks to 'his bond' are

finely relieved by his love for his daughter and his grief for her loss. These various passions were finely portrayed by Mr Powrie, who, without any unnatural striving after effect, made every point tell; not that he wanted fire and spirit, on the contrary, when these were required, he showed he had abundance of the 'thunder which pleaseth the gods', but when he had occasion to use it, he did his 'spiriting gently'. We hail the advent of this gentleman as an era in our theatrical annals, and if he continues as he has begun, he will be an honour to Scotland and an ornament to the British stage.

Tom Powrie by Henry Harwood. *Courtesy of the McManus Galleries, Dundee*

Powrie remained in Glasgow—with regular appearances in Edinburgh and Dundee—for more than ten years, his most frequent parts being Shylock, Iago, Hamlet, Sir Giles Overreach and, of course, Rob Roy. According to Walter Baynham, who acted with Powrie and knew him well, he was a keen student of Scott and was unrivalled as Rob, even though his interpretation of the part was not really original. Powrie had apparently learned the rôle from his first manager, Langley, whose performance was very imitative of Corbet Ryder. Even so, it was Powrie's performance as Rob which led to his one and only London engagement, at Drury Lane in 1861.

This performance, which might have lifted Powrie's career to a higher level, actually signalled the end of it. He played Drury Lane for just one night, after which he had the misfortune to break his ankle and was forced to cancel the remainder of his engagement. He returned to Scotland, settled in Edinburgh and acted only occasionally until his death in 1868, at the early age of 44. According to Baynham, only two people were with Powrie at his death, both of them actors. One of these was Willie Campbell, a Glasgow comedian in the Mackay tradition, who usually played the Bailie to Powrie's Rob. The other was his wife, Juliana Glover, whom Powrie had married in 1860.

If Powrie's exit from the acting profession seems unusually abrupt, the explanation lies in the fact that he had independent means and was, in fact, rather a wealthy man. He owned several businesses and properties in Dundee and possibly had to choose between these committments and a life on the stage. On the other hand, it might well have been that this decision was influenced by a sequence of events which took place at more or less the same time.

In 1860, at the comparatively early age of 47, Edmund Glover died of dropsy at the Edinburgh home of his friend and colleague, Robert Wyndham. Everyone in the Scottish theatre mourned the passing of this fine actor, but the loss was felt most acutely in Glasgow. Glover had been a kind man, full of generosity which he displayed without ostentation. (One of the last acts of his life was to mount a benefit for George Webster, one of the most versatile of his company who had, through illness, fallen on hard times.) At Dunlop Street, he was considered to be irreplaceable.

As it was, the Theatre Royal did not long outlive him. Two years later, in 1862, it was destroyed by a fire which broke out, fortunately enough, during the night while the theatre was empty. Walter Baynham, who was the company stage manager at the time, was roused from his bed and went directly to the theatre where he witnessed a scene that he was later to record in his *History of the Glasgow Stage*.

> The conflagration was at its height, and its flames were visible for miles around. In the ruddy glare, which lit up the dark night and brought to view the dense crowd below, and the scared faces at every window and on every roof above, were to be seen the features of many a patron and many an actor. Prominent on the stone steps leading to the Garrick's Head were the figures of Mr R H Wyndham and Mr George Alexander.

The presence of these two men seems curiously appropriate. George Alexander, old Alick's son, might be said to represent the past while Robert Wyndham could equally claim to represent the future. As such, it seems fitting that they should be present to witness the destruction of the Glasgow Theatre Royal, which signalled the end of an era. The Scottish Theatre was about to enter the darkest night of its entire history.

Chapter Seven

THE STROLLING PLAYERS

In the second half of the nineteenth century, the Scottish Theatre was overtaken by a series of cataclysmic changes—artistic, political, social and even technological in nature—which came close to obliterating it completely. As it was, the sense of a Scottish theatrical tradition was lost so entirely that, when a renaissance eventually occurred—as we shall presently see—its instigators felt as if they were creating something that was completely new.

The most fundamental change of all had to do with the nature of the audience. With the advance of the Industrial Revolution, the population of urban Scotland grew very quickly, due to the emergence of a new working class, many of whom were immigrants from Ireland and the Highlands. It was at this time that theatrical activity began to assume a class dimension, fuelling feelings of alienation on the part of the poor and superiority on the part of the rich. The intensity of this division varied from place to place, but it was particularly acute in Glasgow, with its huge immigrant population and its socially ambitious middle class. As far as the wealthier section of the population was concerned, the following extract from an article in the *Glasgow Dramatic Review* of 1846 expresses the prevailing attitude.

> The respectable portion of the inhabitants, those who are most able to support a theatre, may virtually be said to have none. Ladies cannot be taken to the Adelphi: at Dunlop Street, they are certain to be disgusted by the unlicensed tongue, or the exhibition of buffoonery or imbecility, save when a 'star' appears; and even then the gratification is so qualified, that the desire to return is never felt.

On the other hand, when John Anderson, the so-called 'Wizard of the North' opened his short-lived City Theatre at the foot of the Saltmarket in August 1845, a petition of 60,000 signatures was raised in opposition to this building, claiming that Anderson was infringing the rights of the people to the common land of Glasgow Green. Quite clearly, the poorer classes regarded this huge building—its pit alone held 3,000—as a haunt of the privileged and much trouble was averted when it burned down after only ten weeks' business.

The popular audience created by such as Murray, Alexander, Glover and Mrs Pollock over the past half-century was beginning to break down—but there was more to this than simply class resentment. Much as they might deplore the exclusivity of the rich, the fact is the working classes needed to be exclusive, too. Crammed as they were into overcrowded slums, they had a positive incentive to go out in the evening and needed a form of entertainment that was both cheap and informal.

As the century wore on, this requirement began to be met by the 'free and easies', 'harmony rooms' or 'music halls' that were established in public houses. Throughout the British Isles, such places provided a network for singers, comedians and speciality acts to ply their trade. It was not long before a number of shrewd entrepreneurs came to the conclusion that the future lay in moving these performances into regular theatres. Men like Willie McFarland in Aberdeen and Dundee, Harry Moss in Edinburgh and Willie Campbell in Glasgow opened chains of Music Halls during the 1860s and 70s. In this way, the Variety Theatre was born.

The popularity of Variety obviously affected what came to be known as the 'legitimate' theatre; not only did the Variety theatres draw off part of the audience, they attracted some of the more popular performers, too. As early as 1846, William Murray's American nephew, Sam Cowell—a fine comic actor who had spent several seasons with Murray at the Theatre Royal—found that he could make twice the money for a quarter of the effort by singing comic songs in music halls. Later on, comedians such as R S Pillans and W F Frame—who, a generation earlier, would have found employment as low comedians with stock companies—worked almost exclusively in Variety.

Changes were taking place in the 'legitimate' theatre too. In the early 1860s, a young actress called Marie Wilton borrowed £1,000 from a relative and took over a run-down theatre in Tottenham Court Road in London. After renovation, she opened it as the Prince of Wales Theatre and, in company with her future husband Squire Bancroft and a young playwright called Tom Robertson, she effected a revolution in the English theatre. When the Bancrofts appeared in Tom Robertson's new comedy *Society* on 11 November, 1865, a completely new style of theatre was created, one which would prove not only fashionable but extremely respectable. This new style—it was known as 'cup and saucer' theatre, because of its apparent realism—would attract a middle-class audience as never before.

Six years later, the London theatre experienced another revolutionary event. On 25 November, 1871, at the Lyceum Theatre in the Strand, Henry Irving made his first appearance in the rôle of Matthias in a play by Leopold Lewis called *The Bells*. It was Irving's performance in this play which, in the words of his grandson, 'delivered the English theatre into his hands'. His pre-eminence would last for another 30 years, during which time he would be responsible for raising the art of acting—and of theatrical production generally—to new heights of excellence. Henry Irving, to a greater extent than any other single actor, was responsible for returning the theatre to its artistic roots. He was only able to do this, however, because the policy of the Bancrofts had given the theatre an entirely new status in society at large.

In Scotland, particularly in Edinburgh, these events must have been viewed with a degree of satisfaction. Both Marie Wilton and Henry Irving had received their early training under Wyndham at the Theatre Royal, as had others who would make substantial contributions to the new theatre that was emerging at that time. John Laurence Toole, Edward Compton and Arthur Wing Pinero, all of whom had served their time with Wyndham, would become part of what we can now recognize as a Golden Age.

Yet, ironically enough, it was this very Golden Age—or, rather, the technology that made it possible—which led to the death of the old Scottish theatre. Over the past 30 years, the railway network had gradually been establishing itself throughout the British Isles, making the stock circuit redundant. Henry Irving, unlike his illustrious predecessors, Mrs Siddons, Kean and Macready, would not require to tour alone, playing with stock companies along the way. He could take his entire company—actors, sets, props and costumes—with him as he toured. Nor was Irving alone in this, for the practice would be followed by other London companies. The day of the actor-manager had arrived.

There is no doubt that a glorious chapter in the annals of English-speaking Theatre was written at this time. The demarcation that existed between the West End and the Provinces was suspended and the British Theatre enjoyed a unity such as it had never previously enjoyed. It seemed an appropriate unity, too, for this was the high summer of the British Empire, when the interests of England, Scotland, Ireland and Wales seemed absolutely at one. Since the concerns of the Scottish community were identical to that of the English community, there seemed no reason why they should not be reflected in an all-British Theatre. It is undeniably the case that Irving and the other actor-managers, unlike their counterparts of a century earlier, were never regarded as strangers by Scottish audiences.

The fact remains, however, that the railways gave the London theatre a dominance that it had never enjoyed before and which it has never completely relinquished since. It is entirely due to this comparatively short period that the Scottish Theatre lost its memory. The chain of tradition had been broken and, when the inevitable reaction occurred, the lessons of the past two hundred years would have to be completely re-learned.

As a result of all these changes, the Scottish Theatre simply collapsed. The resident companies were disbanded and the individual theatres either went over to Variety or became receiving houses for the touring actor-managers. As far as Scottish actors were concerned, there was almost no work for them in Scotland and they either had to move to London or give up the stage altogether. Newcomers, of course, had no opportunities in Scotland; actors like Alfred Brydone from Edinburgh, Agnes Fraser from Fife and Norman McKinnel from Kirkcudbright spent their entire careers based in the West End. One curious case was that of Frank Worthing (real name Pentland), who played leading rôles in both London and New York, yet retained his home in the Trinity district of Edinburgh, returning there between seasons. At the other extreme, there was William Mollison from Dundee, who settled in London but made an attempt to retain his roots by organising occasional productions of Scott dramas in partnership with the singer, Durward Lely.

Mostly, though, Scottish actors were content to put Scotland behind them. Many, in fact, were at pains to disguise their background, fearing that they would become typecast and restricted to Scottish parts. Largely as a consequence of this, Scottish writers were unable to take part in the new artistic status that the theatre was beginning to enjoy.

In the latter part of the nineteenth century, there was a quite astonishing resurgence of serious dramatic writing throughout Europe; Ibsen from Norway, Strindberg from Sweden, Chekhov from Russia, Suderman from Germany, Brieux from France and Pinero from England are just a few of the many playwrights who contributed to this movement. The sole Scottish contributor was J M Barrie whose work, for all its quality, was always inhibited by the environment of the London theatre. It could hardly have been otherwise, since it simply was not possible for any Scottish playwright to be produced in Scotland.

Theatrical tradition always dies hard, however, and a few brave spirits made an effort to soldier on. In Edinburgh, at the Theatre Royal—and later at the Royal Lyceum—J B Howard and Fred Wyndham maintained a resident company, the Howard and Wyndham Players, during the summer months. Although the mainstay of their programme was the Waverley Dramas, they did not, interestingly enough, use the old texts but commissioned new versions from playwrights such as Robert Buchanan and Charles Webb. These seasons—which came to an end, at least on a regular basis, with Howard's untimely death in 1895—suffered badly from the dearth of talented actors and Howard was often reduced to casting the office staff.

A similar difficulty was also faced by John Clyde—the last of the great Rob Roys—who toured Scotland, first with the Mollison/Lely company and latterly with his own John Clyde Seasons. Clyde, who had began his working life as a draper in Blairgowrie and took to the stage in Glasgow, involved his whole family in these tours. His daughter, Jean, became a successful West End actress in the 1920s and his two sons, David and Andy—who found international fame as Hopalong Cassidy's sidekick—later made film careers in Hollywood. Although the Clydes were a popular, indeed well-loved, company, they could not possibly compete with the all-round excellence of the London actor-managers.

By the turn of the century, therefore, anything resembling a distinctive Scottish theatre could scarcely be said to exist. There was, of course, the Christmas pantomime, which has a distinct line of development in Scotland. William Murray, it will be remembered, had been trained by Charles Farley, one of the most important pioneers of the modern pantomime. During his years at the Theatre Royal, Murray had modified the lessons he had received from Farley and developed a style to suit his Scottish audience. Murray passed on his expertise to Robert Wyndham, who in turn trained his son, Fred. In the early decades of the twentieth century, Fred Wyndham's sumptuous Glasgow pantomimes would be the last word in colour and spectacle. Even today, in the mixture of magical fairy-tale and down-to-earth topicality that is pantomime, the essential nature of the old Scottish theatre can still be seen.

Pantomime aside, however, there was little else. National Drama, if not exactly dead and buried, was living in very reduced circumstances. There was a species of fit-up company, known as the 'penny geggie', which toured country districts which were beyond the reach of the conventional theatres and where the old style of theatre still held some appeal. Joe Corrie, in a posthumously published talk on the subject, remembers seeing the young Will Fyffe appearing with one of these companies in a play called *Burke and Hare*. He also recalls the demise of this company.

> The season of the Penny Geggie was nearing its end. In two weeks time the players would pack their belongings and silently steal away. We would miss them, but wish them God speed and good luck. Alas, we didn't have that pleasure. One night a hurricane rose and blew so fiercely that we all spent a sleepless and apprehensive night. When daylight broke there was no Penny Geggie to be seen; it had been blown asunder and the construction, the scenery, the props, everything was being washed down the river, never to be rescued. Those who were unmarried packed their few belongings and made their way slowly to the railway station, not knowing where or when they would again strut the stage. But those who were married and had children hadn't the means to go. But they were befriended by the village folk and heartily welcomed to share what little there was to share in those days.

In the towns, the penny geggies had their counterparts in a low kind of theatre known as the 'penny gaff'. These had something in common with the 'free and easies' in that they were usually situated in the back room of a public house. In place of stand-up comedy and popular song, National Drama, Shakespeare and original poems and monologues were presented. At a famous penny gaff in Blackfriars Wynd, Edinburgh, James Lumsden would perform his poems and songs, actors such as George Fisher and Lizzie Wilmore would perform extracts from the Scott plays as well as the monologues of James Smith, while the star of the evening was always the colourful Edinburgh bohemian, Ned Holt, who would perform scenes from *Hamlet*.

Then there was the concert platform. In the days before recording and broadcasting, musical evenings were presented nightly throughout the Scottish cities. A feature of these concerts was the elocutionist, who would recite poems, monologues and extracts from novels—known as 'national readings'—between the musical items.

One of the most popular elocutionists of the late Victorian age was a young man from Innerleithen called William Moffat, whose speciality was reciting extracts from the popular Scottish novelist, Norman MacLeod. However, since it was not really possible to earn a living from the concert platform, Moffat supplemented his income by teaching. He wrote a book on his subject—entitled simply, if unoriginally, *Moffat's Elocution*—and set up practice in Sauchiehall Street, Glasgow, where his pupils included politicians, ministers of religion and others who were called upon to speak in public. His business prospered and together with his wife, the former Helen Dobson, he raised a remarkable family of four sons and two daughters. The boys—known, in the Lowland Scottish custom, by their middle names—were Dickson, Sanderson, Graham and Watson. The girls were Catherine and Helen.

All of William Moffat's children became actors. Dickson Moffat, the eldest, was a comedian in the Charles Mackay tradition and played the Bailie on a number of occasions with the Durward Lely company. Unfortunately, his early death deprived him of the experience of working with his siblings. In the first decades of the twentieth century, the Moffats would form the basis of the most successful and widely-travelled theatre company that Scotland has ever produced.

Their father's slightly unusual occupation notwithstanding, the Moffats were a fairly typical Lowland Scottish family of the time. Every Sunday, they were regularly seen at Elgin Place Congregational Church, where the parents were members and the children attended Sunday School. Although William Moffat made his living by teaching the correct enunciation of Received Standard English, he ensured that his children had a wide knowledge of Scottish literature and the language of the home was invariably Scots. Only one generation removed from the land, the Moffats inherited all the shrewd wisdom of the Scots peasant. This was particularly true of Mrs Moffat, whose conversation was laced with proverbs and pithy sayings. 'Aim at a silk goun' she once told her third son 'and ye'll aye get the sleeve o't'.

The young man to whom this remark was addressed was possessed of abundant energy, many enthusiasms, inspired organisational ability and more than his fair share of theatrical talent. Graham Moffat, born in Glasgow in 1866, would prove to be the driving force of the family's future.

After an uncomfortable education at Glasgow's Rosemount Academy, Graham found a job as a office boy but quickly realised that there was no future for him in a business career. Deciding to follow in his father's footsteps, he studied his father's teaching methods and took over the practice on his father's death. Besides working in Glasgow, he also spent some time in Dundee, where he taught elocution to divinity students at St Andrew's University. Like his father before him, he supplemented his income with appearances on the concert platform—sometimes on his own, sometimes with his sister Kate—and by working as a photographer in the summer months, supplying landscapes for the makers of picture postcards. In 1897, he met and married Margaret Liddell Linck.

The marriage of Graham and Maggie Moffat was a true partnership in every sense of the word. They did everything together and the enthusiasm of one was automatically supported and encouraged by the other. When Maggie became involved in the Suffrage Movement—she was a follower of Charlotte Despard and was jailed for two weeks after attending an illegal meeting in 1906—Graham gave her his immediate and whole-hearted support. He organised 'The Glasgow Men's League for Women's Suffrage' and led them at demonstrations and marches in Glasgow and Edinburgh. They had a banner which read

Men's League for Women's Suffrage
Scots What Hae Votes—Men
Scots What Haenna—Women!

Maggie, for her part, threw her support behind Graham in all his enterprises, most notably one which began towards the end of 1907.

In the late summer of that year, the Abbey Theatre of Dublin paid a visit to Glasgow with two plays: *Cathleen ni Houlihan* by W B Yeats and *The Well of the Saints* by J M Synge. More than 40 years later, in his autobiography *Join Me In Remembering* (1955), Graham Moffat would acknowledge the effect that this had on his theatrical ambitions. Inspired by the Abbey, Moffat deliberately set out to create a Scottish theatre along similar lines.

Since the Abbey was essentially a writers' theatre company, promoting new, indigenous drama, Moffat's first act was to write a play. The popular Scottish song *Annie Laurie*—and the tragic story that lay behind it—was the basis of Moffat's first attempt, a serious drama. In order to balance the programme with some light relief, Moffat then wrote a comedy, *Till the Bells Ring*. With the help of Maggie and the other members of his family, a company was formed to produce both plays. The name that Moffat gave this company had a curiously prophetic ring: he called it The Scottish National Players.

They opened at the Athenaeum Theatre, Glasgow, on 26 March, 1908. *Annie Laurie* did not make much of an impact—Moffat never seems to have played it again—but the comedy was an immediate success. W G Robb, an old Scottish actor who attended that performance, was heard to snort that 'Moffat never wrote that play—he stole it from Barrie!' Far from being dismayed by this comment—which he regarded as a compliment—Moffat felt enough encouragement to write and produce two more plays: a one-act farce entitled *The Concealed Bed* and a full-length comedy, *A Scrape o' the Pen*.

Meanwhile, others in Glasgow had found similar inspiration from the visit of the Abbey Theatre. In 1909, a group of enthusiasts formed a new company, Scottish Playgoers Ltd, whose prospectus included the following aim:

The objects of the company include...the encouragement of the initiation and development of purely Scottish drama by providing a stage and acting company which will be peculiarly adapted for the production of plays national in character, written by Scottish men and women of letters.

Norman MacOwan, Agnes Miller and Graham Moffat in *A Scrape o' the Pen*
Courtesy of Edinburgh City Library

The wording of that statement raises two points that it would be as well to deal with immediately. First, the phrase 'initiation and development' suggests that a revival of the old Scottish theatre was not what the board of Scottish Playgoers had in mind. (Indeed, it is doubtful if these people even knew that such a theatre had ever existed; almost 50 years, after all, had passed since the destruction of the Dunlop Street Theatre Royal.) Secondly, the declared intention of creating a 'purely Scottish drama' was to prove to be extremely misleading. Far from promoting a genuinely indigenous drama, it soon became clear that the ambitions of the Scottish Playgoers were much more in line with the attitude of the anonymous contributor to *The Glasgow Dramatic Review*, quoted above. The new company was not devoted to the Scottish audience at large but to 'the respectable portion of the inhabitants, those who are most able to support a theatre'.

The board of Scottish Playgoers was composed, for the most part, of people who had little knowledge of theatre. Professors W McNeile Dixon and J S

Phillimore were academics at the University of Glasgow where they held the Chairs of English and Humanities respectively. Deacon Convenor Andrew Macdonald was a businessman, J W Robb was a chartered accountant, Neil Munro was a journalist and only Alfred Wareing, who was to be responsible for productions, had any theatrical experience.

It is strange how often history seems to repeat itself. To no lesser extent than the Elibank group in Edinburgh 150 years earlier, these Glasgow worthies probably thought that they had found the best man for the job. Alfred Wareing, after all, had been responsible for the British tour which had brought the Abbey Theatre to Glasgow in 1907. Furthermore, he had worked as a business manager for the touring companies of Frank Benson and Herbert Beerbohm Tree. All things considered, Wareing seemed to be a man who knew his business, one who could be trusted to give the new company the best possible start. Unfortunately, like the Elibank group before them, the board of Scottish Playgoers Ltd were to be profoundly disappointed.

Despite his connection with the Abbey Theatre, Wareing had little interest in native drama. Nor had his work with Benson and Tree allowed any of the colourful flamboyance of these great actor-managers to have any influence on his approach. When he announced his first season, he did so with all the panache and rhetorical flourish of a retail chemist or purveyor of dry goods.

The Glasgow Repertory Theatre is Glasgow's own theatre, financed by Glasgow, managed by Glasgow men. Established to make Glasgow independent of London for its Dramatic supplies, it is a Citizen's Theatre in the fullest sense of the term.

An abrupt change of policy can immediately be noted. Instead of being devoted to 'the initiation and development of a purely Scottish drama', the aim is now to create 'Glasgow's own theatre'. The concern of the company, moreover, is not with 'plays national in character' but simply with the vague and perfectly grotesque concept of 'dramatic supplies'. Worse, however, was to follow. In his programme note for the company's first production—Shaw's *You Never Can Tell*—Wareing made a rather quaint attack on the old stock system (which had disappeared from Scotland a generation earlier and was almost beyond living memory) and announced his intention of producing 'ultra-modern playwrights like Bernard Shaw, John Galsworthy and Arnold Bennett'. A member of Scottish Playgoers in 1909 might reasonably have been expected to ask what happened to those 'Scottish men and women of letters' who were supposed to contribute to the new enterprise.

From the first, Wareing pursued a policy that flew in the face of the *declared* policy of Scottish Playgoers. He made no attempt to create a resident company, far less one that would be 'peculiarly adapted for the production of plays national in character'. Except in minor rôles, he employed no Scottish actors and cast his production from the ranks of out-of-work members of the touring companies. Mary Jerrold and Hubert Harben came from the Kendal company,

94

Franklin Dyall from George Alexander, Madge McIntosh from Edward Compton, Harold Chapin from Frank Benson, Creagh Henry from Ben Greet and Frederick Sargent from Mrs Patrick Campbell. Since few of these actors remained for more than one or two plays, it was impossible for the company even to begin to develop any sort of relationship with the Glasgow audience.

Not to put too fine a point upon it, Wareing's management was characterised by feckless incompetence. Even at a simple business level, he was woefully inadequate. (The average theatre rent in 1909 was £25; Wareing cheerfully paid more than three times that much for the Royalty in Sauchiehall Street.) Although he kept making confident pronouncements regarding the company's welfare, the truth is that the Glasgow Rep was operating at a serious loss. Over the four years of its history, the investment of Scottish Playgoers suffered to the tune of £6,000.

Wareing's saving grace would appear to have been his play policy. Viewed from a historical perspective, his record in this respect does seem quite impressive. His rôle-model was clearly the Vedrenne-Barker management in London, whose ground-breaking seasons at London's Royal Court had proved a substantial critical success. Vedrenne-Barker, however, had been operating in the greatest theatrical centre of all, where there was a long and distinguished theatrical tradition and a much larger and more sympathetic audience—and, even then, had barely succeeded in breaking even. Their critical success could not possibly hope to be repeated in Glasgow, with its record of hostility towards the legitimate stage. Nevertheless, the Glasgow Rep's productions of Chekhov—the first by a British company—Shaw, Ibsen and other contemporary dramatists suggests that there was a brave and adventurous spirit at the helm. Unfortunately, quite the opposite was the case. The truth is that Wareing was never more than a superficial imitator who was, at heart, artistically timid. This timidity was to cost the Scottish Theatre dear.

Although Wareing had little knowledge of or interest in Scottish drama, there were occasions when he had to pay lip service to local sensibilities. One of these was the Christmas show, which was always expected to have a Scottish dimension. In 1910, Wareing's musical director Albert Cazabon, together with a writer called G J Hamlin produced an adaptation of George McDonald's story, *The Carasoyn*, to which they gave the title *Colin in Fairyland*. Graham and Maggie Moffat were engaged by Wareing to play the parts of McTavish and Lucky McGraw in this production.

At this time, Moffat had just completed a new play. Entitled *Causay Saints*, it was a comic satire on the theme of Sabbatarianism and Moffat thought that it might be right for the Glasgow Rep. Wareing, to his credit, showed some interest in the play and promised to consider it for production after the run of *Colin in Fairyland*. Unfortunately, during the opening performances of the Christmas show, an incident took place which made any such production impossible.

The parts that Graham and Maggie Moffat were given to play were quite small, but they did have one very funny scene involving some business with an egg-box and three lines of dialogue. For some obscure reason, these three lines gave offence to a member of the audience, who wrote to the papers in complaint. Wareing's response to this was to order that these lines be cut from the show. Since this made nonsense of his performance, Moffat protested, quoting the old theatrical maxim that 'every laugh is worth fifty pounds of business'. Wareing, however, was adamant—these three lines of dialogue would have to go. In an attempt at compromise, Moffat substituted three (presumably less offensive) lines of his own. Wareing was furious. He presented Moffat with an ultimatum: either cut these lines or face dismissal. Moffat was equally furious. He did not see why he should lose a perfectly good performance just because one member of the audience had written to the papers. He accepted dismissal quite happily and when he went to the office with Maggie to collect their wages, Wareing's copy of *Causay Saints* was returned to him. This was the first link in a chain of events which would lead to a theatrical sensation.

Graham and Maggie were not long out of work. They auditioned at the Empress Music Hall in St George's Cross and were immediately given a spot on the bill, playing the *The Concealed Bed*. It was while playing at the Empress that they were spotted by a representative of the London booking agents, Somers and Warner, who signed them up for a season on the Barrasford circuit of London Music Halls. In addition to this, while playing at the London Pavilion, Somers and Warner arranged for Moffat's earlier Glasgow success, *Till the Bells Ring* to have a matinee performance at the Royalty Theatre with a view to attracting trade interest. Attending this matinee was a senior partner in the firm, Ben Nathan.

A Glaswegian by birth, Nathan might well have known the Moffats before this, for he had begun, like Graham Moffat, as a platform performer in Scotland. In any event, he took an immediate interest in the work of the company. On the morning after this matinee, Nathan was crossing Trafalgar Square when he happened to meet the actor-manager Cyril Maude, then running the Playhouse Theatre in Northumberland Avenue. In the course of their conversation, Maude mentioned that he was looking for a good light comedy and Nathan quickly took the opportunity to put Moffat in touch with Maude.

The two men hit it off immediately. Moffat read *Till the Bells Ring* to the London manager, who liked it so much that he booked Moffat to appear in it at the Playhouse. This did not solve his original problem, however, since he had been looking for a comedy that would provide a vehicle for himself. When he asked Moffat if he had any other plays, Moffat suggested *Causay Saints*. Maude seemed a little doubtful at first, but asked for a reading. 'I'll do better than that!' cried Moffat enthusiastically, 'I'll play it for you!'.

A matinee was arranged at the Playhouse for the following week. Luckily, all Moffat's family—plus one or two other Scottish actors he needed to complete the cast—were present in London at the time and *Causay Saints* was quickly rehearsed and played with quite astonishing success. By the following day, Moffat had received offers from no fewer than five London managements for *Causay*

Saints. Appreciative of the help he had received from Maude, however, Moffat refused to consider any of them unless the actor-manager of the Playhouse gave him a release. Cyril Maude, who was as wise as he was generous, knew that the place for the play was the Haymarket and he suggested that Moffat accept the offer he had received from Herbert Trench of that theatre. He also made an additional suggestion, one which was to prove significant. The play's title, Maude felt, was much too Scottish for London and offered an alternative. Towards the end of the play, one of the characters declares: 'That's oor Bunty! Aye pullin' the strings!

In this way, *Causay Saints* became *Bunty Pulls the Strings* and it was under the new title that the play opened at the Haymarket on 11 July, 1911. W Macqueen-Pope, who was present on the occasion, gives a description of that evening in his *Haymarket : Theatre of Perfection* (1948).

> Trench took a chance—a very daring chance. He brought to the smart, distinguished Haymarket Theatre a play and a company of players which had never expected to come to London at all, let alone to the Haymarket. The play was a Scots comedy, the players all Scots. It was all in dialect and concerned Lowland Scots of humble birth and degree. It did not seem the thing at all. Nobody had heard of anyone in the cast...An almost unwilling audience attended. The stalls and the circle expected to be bored, while the cheaper gentry anticipated having to register disapproval. For plays in the Scots vernacular were not popular as a rule. Even the romantic Highlands did not get across the footlights too well, and this was an affair of parlours and kirkyards. There was doubt and trepidation. But that play succeeded. Such real life, such observation, such situations, such pungent and homely wit, so well told a story and so well played, it swept to success. It had its audience standing up and cheering.

They cheered for a total of 20 curtain calls and the play enjoyed a run of no fewer than 617 performances, keeping the company at the Haymarket until 1912. Moffat then followed up this success with his earlier Scots comedy, *A Scrape o' the Pen*, which ran for another two years at the nearby Comedy Theatre. In April, 1914, the company embarked for Australia and for the next decade—with the exception of a short engagement at the Glasgow Alhambra in 1920—they played all over the English-speaking world, visiting Australia, the United States and Canada (twice) and South Africa.

Throughout the '20s, the Moffats played exclusively in London and did not return to Scotland until 1932 when, for only the second time in his life, Graham Moffat took the stage in a rôle (or rather rôles) that had not come from his own pen. To celebrate Sir Walter Scott's centenary, Howard and Wyndham produced a season of Waverley Dramas, in which Moffat played all the characters he had known since boyhood: Davie Deans, Dominie Sampson and Bailie Nicol Jarvie. Although this season was not a success—the old texts had become horribly dated—Moffat always regarded these performances as representing the high point of his acting career.

Retiring in 1936, the Moffats emigrated to South Africa where Graham spent his declining years in the study of another enthusiasm: spiritualism. This produced a rather interesting book, *Towards Eternal Day : The Psychic Memoirs of a Playwright*, which appeared in 1948. His theatrical memoirs, *Join Me in Remembering*, appeared shortly after his death in 1955.

From the point of view of Scottish theatre history, the success of the Moffat company must be regarded with mixed feelings. On one hand, there can be no doubt that Moffat's work achieved a palpable victory for his vision of a genuinely Scottish style of theatre. In spite of suggestions to the contrary—which always infuriated him—he never compromised to suit the tastes of the London audience. (In this respect, the change of title, made at Cyril Maude's suggestion, has done much long-term damage. *Bunty Pulls the Strings,* with its inevitable echo of a dated form of schoolgirl fiction, gives a completely misleading impression of Moffat's play.) Circumstances may have induced the Moffat company to become strolling players, but as far as they were concerned, they continued to remain true to the inspiration Graham Moffat had received from the visit of the Abbey Theatre in 1907.

On the other hand, it is equally true that the Haymarket success robbed the Scottish Theatre of its most talented and productive company. There is considerable irony in the fact that this loss should be suffered at a time when leading citizens of Scotland's largest city were campaigning for just such a company. The question must be asked: why did the Moffats not achieve at least part of their success in Glasgow? Part of the blame, of course, must lie with Alfred Wareing, but it would be over-simplistic—and not a little unfair—to suggest that Moffat left Scotland because Wareing would not allow him to get a laugh at the Royalty.

The fact is that, had Scottish Playgoers Ltd. been seriously committed to the original principles of their manifesto, as quoted above, they would have encouraged Moffat's company from the start. If, instead of squandering their resources on Alfred Wareing's fruitless and foolhardy attempt to emulate Harley Granville Barker, they had invested in Moffat's Scottish National Players, the success of *Bunty Pulls the Strings*—which would, in such an event, have been known by its original title, *Causay Saints*—might very easily have been achieved in Glasgow as well as in London. Although it is not, of course, possible to be sure of this, the least that can with certainty be said is that, if such a policy had been in force, the emerging Scottish Theatre would have been placed on a much firmer footing.

As it was, the Glasgow Repertory Theatre came to an end with the outbreak of the First World War and, when hostilities ceased, there was little incentive to revive the company. Scottish Playgoers Ltd was wound up and the residual funds transferred to the St Andrews Society of Glasgow, who would later make use of them to initiate another, quite different, theatrical venture. All that survived of the Glasgow Rep, unfortunately, was the attitude that had fostered and informed it: a compound of unconfessed ignorance, a profound lack of confidence and overweening social pretensions. It is a species of artistic élitism that would do much damage over the years.

Fortunately for the Scottish Theatre, there were other forces at work which were more than capable of transcending its destructive influence.

Chapter Eight

JOE CORRIE AND THE AMATEURS

There are nineteen streets in our village, long rows of houses—all alike in plan and style. The roads between them are carpeted with mud.

On the height to the west there is a blaze of light, a hissing of steam, and a screeching of machinery. The great wheels turn, halt, and turn again, and the clang of the signals can be heard in every home. The dreariest place on earth, this colliery village on a winter night.

In a kitchen in the centre of the hamlet a small group of men and women sit with papers in their hands reading aloud. Now and again, a voice bursts into song. They are rehearsing a play.

A mother of five sings an old Scottish song with a sincerity that many a prima donna would envy. The 'funny part' is in the hands of a little man who need not act at all to bring tears of laughter to our eyes. The lover's part is being spoken by a young man who broke the law for the sake of industrial solidarity. He is newly home after his term of imprisonment.

On the great night they will play, in the full glare of the footlights, and the audience, for at least one evening, will forget its slavery and mock its 'maisters' with the ripping laughter of youth.

These are the words of the most beloved and, in many ways, the most influential of all Scottish playwrights—Joe Corrie. They are an expression both of his background and of the entire purpose of his work. Although his reputation is that of a radical, left-wing, essentially political playwright, it would be a gross oversimplification to regard him simply as such. Joe Corrie lived through a time of great political moment and neither his artistic integrity nor the experience of his upbringing would allow him to be other than political. Yet there is much that transcends politics in his work, which at times takes on an almost spiritual dimension. Throughout his professional career, he remained true to the ideals of Community Drama—plays created out of community experience, for performance by community actors to a community audience—and, as such, his loyalty remained consistently with the Amateur Movement.

The Amateur Theatre has a long history in Scotland, having its roots in school and church drama. During the period covered by this book, however, its development was given considerable stimulus by the work of the professional companies. This was particularly true in the smaller towns and villages covered by the touring circuits during the nineteenth century. Since such as Alexander in the south-west and the Ryders in the north-east were restricted by law to playing very short seasons, this meant that the buildings in which they performed were often under-used. These legal restrictions did not apply to amateurs—or, at the very least, could be easily circumvented by them—and this led to much amateur activity.

Many Scottish amateur companies have a very long record of continuous production. The Dumfries Guild of Players, for instance, can trace its history right back to the time of Robert Burns. On the other side of the country, there was a thriving amateur theatre in Arbroath for much of the nineteenth century. (This company even had its own star, a local auctioneer called George Rutherford Thomson, who was so popular that he was sometimes engaged to draw business by the professional company in Dundee.) These instances, moreover, were far from being exceptional. J Keith Angus, in his *A Scotch Play-house* tells us that 'A glance at the pages of the *Era* will show that nearly every place of consequence throughout the country, even so far north as Lerwick, has its permanent or improvised theatre open.'

Most of these theatres were occupied by local amateur companies, who provided theatrical entertainment in the places that the touring companies could not reach.

After the First World War—for reasons that will be discussed more fully in a later chapter—a quite phenomenal upsurge in amateur activity took place throughout the British Isles. The British Drama League, founded by Geoffrey Whitworth in 1919, attracted no fewer than 2,500 member-companies in its first ten years of existence. This growth was largely stimulated by competitive festivals, which were often viewed with disdain by professionals. Whitworth defended these festivals, however, on the grounds that while 'the highest art may not be found as result of competition, at least it is a safeguard against the worst'. In an article which appeared in *Theatre and Stage* in 1932, Whitworth also expressed the philosophy of the movement.

> The moral exhaustion that was the aftermath of the War has left mankind at the mercy of the mechanical-economic elements in modern civilization. These elements have given us, it is true, certain alleviations from themselves. The motor-car takes the town dweller into the country with an ease and celerity hitherto unknown. Wireless and radio have opened up for the multitude a new field of dramatic enjoyment, albeit at one or two removes. But these last are purely passive pleasures, and a little tainted at the source. In the main we are still the victims of an impulse which, if pushed to its logical conclusion, would deny to us all that sense of personal vitality which is a prime condition of happiness. Here Drama comes to the rescue. It provides just the needed antidote to the poison of the Machine. On the stage, a free wind of the spirit blows.

There was a moral dimension, therefore, to the new Amateur Movement which found an immediate response in Scotland. The Scottish Community Drama Association (SCDA), founded in 1926, had 35 companies taking part in its first festival. Within a decade, this number had swollen to 1,000, comprising upwards of 25,000 amateur players. This led to a radical reassessment of the place of theatre in Scottish society, which is why many writers on the subject have been misled into the belief that the history of Scottish Theatre only began at this time.

One company which certainly held this belief was the Scottish National Players. In 1921, the St Andrew's Society of Glasgow made use of the residual funds of the defunct Glasgow Rep to stage seasons of new Scottish one-act plays. By the following year, an independent company had been formed and the Players began their work of developing a new Scottish Drama. Although amateur in composition, the Players were totally dedicated to their ideals and, in most respects, thoroughly professional in their approach. Under the direction of a professional resident producer, they performed in the old home of the Glasgow Rep, the Royalty in Sauchiehall Street, now re-named the Lyric.

The first resident producer was A P Wilson of the Abbey Theatre in Dublin. A disciple of Frank and Willie Fay, Wilson was wholly committed to the acting style that the Fay brothers had pioneered at the Abbey; a style in which stillness and the musicality of speech takes precedence over movement and visual effects. It was this form of performance which had been the key to the Abbey's success, but it was most inappropriate for the Scottish National Players. The Scottish love of language is every bit as profound as that of the Irish, but it is of a completely different character, more to do with argument and debate than with poetry and music—Scots are interested in what words *say*, rather than how they *sound*. Although the company inevitably had a number of other problems in these early days, one suspects that Wilson's approach was not greatly appreciated by Scottish audiences, who probably felt patronized by it. In any event, these early productions—of John Brandane's Highland comedy *The Glen is Mine* and Gordon Bottomley's poetic drama *Gruach*—made little impact.

Wilson was replaced as resident producer, first by Frank Clewlow of Birmingham in 1925 and a year later, most significantly, by a gigantic young Irishman from Belfast who had been working as a producer for the fledgling BBC—William Tyrone Guthrie.

Then at the beginning of a brilliant theatrical career—which would earn him a knighthood, a hatful of academic awards and a theatre in Canada to commemorate his name—Tyrone Guthrie arrived like a breath of fresh air. His Irish origins notwithstanding, he had strong Scottish connections in his ancestry. On his father's side, his great-grandfather had been the famous social reformer, Dr Thomas Guthrie of the Free St John's Church in Edinburgh, founder of the 'ragged schools' and one of the most spell-binding preachers of his time. On his mother's side, he was the great-grandson of Tyrone Power, a leading actor of the 1820s, who had once been a member of the Ryder company on the Northern Circuit. A younger cousin of the same name would later become famous in Hollywood for his dashing, swashbuckling rôles—and something of this adventurous spirit was brought to Guthrie's work with the Scottish National Players.

It was Guthrie, in fact, who made the innovation for the which the Scottish National Players are best remembered. With the help of the Carnegie Trust, he organised a tour of small towns and villages in the north of Scotland. A company of seven actors with a caravan and a lorry played a programme of one-act plays, mimed ballads and folk-songs in a series of one-night stands. Sets, costumes and props were kept to the absolute minimum, the company slept under canvas and everybody mucked in. In his letters home, Guthrie tells how Nell Buchanan did the cooking while C R M Brookes looked after the tents; the lighting man, Archie Frew, drove the lorry and Ethel Lewis, who provided another car, looked after the wardrobe; Elliot Mason was in charge of props, Moultrie Kelsall handled stage management, and front-of-house duties—selling programmes and showing people to their seats—were the responsibility of whoever was not in the first act of the play.

Besides initiating these tours, Guthrie also helped to advertise the company through his radio work. Aided by David Cleghorn Thomson, Regional Controller of the BBC in Scotland and a member of the Players' board, he made a number of broadcasts with the company. Having heard the Players on the air, people were interested to see how they looked in the flesh, and audience levels rose accordingly.

During Guthrie's time in Glasgow, he produced eight new Scottish plays, mostly of an ephemeral nature, by writers like Neil Grant, Morland Graham and Cormac Simpson. He soon found, however, that the supply of new Scottish plays was very limited indeed. As noted in the previous chapter, Scottish-based writers were unable to take part in the great resurgence of serious dramatic writing that took place in the latter part of the nineteenth century. Even if this had not been the case, however, the existence of a Scottish repertoire would not *in itself* have solved the problem. The ideals of the British Drama League—to which the Players broadly subscribed—suggested a break with the past and a completely new kind of play was required. The problem, therefore, was not unique to the Scottish National Players and presented a similar difficulty to English companies.

In England, however, the greater degree of theatrical activity had led to the development of a well defined play-writing profession. In London, the actor-managers had employed playwrights as theatrical functionaries whose job was to prepare scripts for performance, tailoring them to the requirements of their particular casts. Writers such as W G Wills—who worked almost exclusively for Irving at the Lyceum—had no great literary ambition but became highly skilled in dramaturgical technique. At the very least, this meant that new English dramatists were able to draw upon an existing tradition.

This situation did not of course obtain in Scotland, where such theatrical functionaries were unknown. It is probably for this reason that the Players became overly concerned with the technical excellence of the plays they performed, at the expense of their social, political or, indeed, artistic content. One writer who had a major influence on play policy—he might be described as the unofficial dramaturg of the Scottish National Players—was John Brandane, whose plays were written exclusively for the company. Brandane's comedies are all set in the Highlands, take a decidedly romantic, not to say conservative, view of Highland life, and are somewhat sterile in terms of any kind of social or political commitment. Without exception, however, Brandane's plays are beautifully constructed models of technical excellence.

Joe Corrie approached the theatre from a completely different direction. A miner to trade, self-educated and raised in the grinding poverty of the West Fife coalfield, Corrie's writing drew its inspiration from the industrial struggles of his time. Although born in the village of Slammanan 1894, he grew up in the Cardenden area of Fife, where his father worked as a surfaceman. At the age of 14, he went to work at the Bowhill pit and for the next 20 years or so he worked as a miner, both below and above ground. His education was of course rudimentary—a basic schooling, supplemented by attendance at Workers' Education Association classes—but not nearly as neglible as it might, at first sight, appear. One of the few good things that the private mine-owners did for their workers was to ensure that there was a well-stocked library at each of the Miners' Institutes. Corrie, a voracious reader, was not slow to take advantage of this, but he was by no means the only miner to do so. In those days, there was a hunger for, and a love of, knowledge among working people which would surprise many in more affluent times. Corrie therefore had the benefit of growing up among a class of people who, despite their economic circumstances, had a profound respect for the written and spoken word. When his first poems appeared, shortly after the First World War, in the local paper, the *Lochgelly Times*, they made an immediate impression. A little later, the Miner's Reform Union paid him £3 a week for a fortnightly contribution to their own publication, *The Miner*.

Corrie's interest in theatre dates from his childhood. An early influence—as noted in the previous chapter—was the 'penny geggies'. One such company was run by a family called Thomas, who first set up their tent at Bowhill farm in 1910. For the next ten years, the Thomases toured throughout Scotland, using Cardenden as their base. According to local information, Corrie was friendly with the Thomas family and often helped with the stage management.

In 1924, Corrie joined the Auchterderran Dramatic Club and appeared in several of their productions. Interviewed in 1986, the founder of that club, R S Gilfillan, remembered Corrie's 'quaint, pawky, manner. He portrayed the characters so nicely...he lived the parts'. By this time, however, he had already begun to write the one-act plays that were to make him famous.

The industrial struggles of the time, with which he was deeply involved, naturally affected his writing. In fact, the writing and production of his first work for the stage was done with the specific purpose of raising money for soup kitchens during the General Strike in 1926. Together with his sister, Violet, his

Joe Corrie
Courtesy of Morag Corrie

two brothers, Jimmy and Bobby, and a number of other miners and their wives, he formed the Bowhill Players to tour his plays throughout Fife. His first published play, *Hogmanay*, was written for the same purpose.

In early 1927, Corrie completed *In Time o' Strife*, his first full-length play, which deals with the effect of the General Strike on an ordinary mining community. This was unquestionably his finest work to date, and Corrie himself was certainly aware of that. Instead of staging it with the Bowhill Players, he immediately submitted the play to the Reading Committee of the Scottish National Players.

He had been encouraged to do so by the Players' successful production of two of his one-act plays, *The Poacher* and *The Shillin' a Week Man*, which had been toured throughout Scotland in 1926. This probably led Corrie to believe that *In Time o' Strife* would receive a sympathetic hearing and, indeed, at first this did seem to be the case. The play was returned to Corrie with some suggestions for improvement, with which Corrie complied. After re-writing, he submitted *In Time o' Strife* again. After a second reading, it was turned down flat.

This was to prove to be a serious mistake on the part of the Players. Convinced of the play's quality, Corrie immediately produced it with his own company. On 28 March, 1928, the following notice appeared in the *Lochgelly Times*:

> The Village Players have been doing much hard work during the winter, visiting the towns and villages of the county, their second visit to Kirkcaldy resulting in 200 people being turned away. Most of their shows in the small villages have resulted in financial loss due to small halls, and it is to recuperate the club for next winter when they intend visiting places outside the county with plays which show the true side of mining life, that they are giving the two shows at Bowhill.

The two shows in question took place in the Gothenburg Hall, Bowhill, and it was here that they were first seen by a variety artist turned theatrical agent called Hugh Ogilvie. Ogilvie had been appearing in a variety show at the Dunfermline Opera House when he heard of the company's success and immediately decided to see them on their home ground. After seeing the first act of *In Time o' Strife*, he lost no time in offering the company representation under his management. As a matter of fact, he was so excited with the potential of what he had seen that he made a public announcement at the end of the performance in which he revealed his enthusiasm for both company and play.

Under Ogilvie, the Bowhill Players were re-constituted as the Fife Miner Players. Apart from Ogilvie and his sons, Benny and George—who handled stage management—they were all miners or people from the mining community, with no grandiose notions of 'the initiation and development of purely Scottish drama' or, indeed, any theatrical ambitions whatsoever, other than to perform with as much truth and conviction as they possibly could. Under Corrie's strict and detailed direction, they succeeded in doing this in a quite remarkable manner.

In 1928, *In Time o' Strife* (with *The Poacher* also on the bill) toured the leading Variety theatres in Aberdeen, Ayr, Coatbridge, Dundee, Dunfermline, Edinburgh, Falkirk, Greenock, Hamilton, Kilmarnock, Leith, Paisley, Perth and Stirling. In all these places—where they played to audiences of approaching a thousand people per night—they were received with enthusiastic acclaim. It was the triumphant success of this tour which established Corrie's reputation as the leading Scottish playwright of his time.

A writer—or a director—can only take a play so far, however. A substantial share of the credit for the success of *In Time o' Strife* must go to Corrie's talented cast. During the Joe Corrie Festival, which was held at the Bowhill Institute in September 1986, some of the surviving members of the Fife Miners gathered to recall their memories of that tour. Most of the talk, of course, was of Joe Corrie, but there was one other name that loomed large in the conversation: Margaret McLean, who played Jean, the mother of the family in *In Time o' Strife*. This huge woman, herself a miner's wife—and mother of five children—brought a powerful authenticity to the rôle. Lizzie Galloway, a member of the company who was only a teenager at the time, remembered Margaret McLean's talent— and her temperament.

> She was great, what a memory she had! See the comedians on the Variety? She could even remember their words as well. She picked up awfully quick. She could cry real...she really cried, carried away with it at times. She loved *The Poacher*. Her under-study, she always declared she wouldn't be able to do it. She was right! The day Mrs McLean didn't turn up, that understudy wasn't able to go on...they had to change the programme.
> She was always drinking...she added on when she got a drink. She never forgot anything, she ad-libbed on...She used to cast out with all of them a lot of the time. She cast out with everybody but me. She walked out one time, and she had George Ogilvie up to ninety! But she came back again. She seen the big queue, and she came back.

While it is virtually certain that such a temperament would have been unac-ceptable to the Scottish National Players, it is extremely doubtful if such a par-ticular talent would have been available to the company at that time. If this thought, however, would appear to justify the decision of the Reading Commit-tee, Joe Corrie did not see it that way. In a letter to the *Daily Record* in October 1929, he accused the Scottish National Players of rejecting *In Time o' Strife* on political grounds.

Whether or not this was truly the case—and class divisions almost certainly played a part in the decision—the context in which this accusation was made is an interesting one. The Players had just produced a play called *The Ancient Fire* by Neil Gunn, a brave attempt to do something experimental with the company. It was, unfortunately, altogether too experimental for its time and failed disastrously with both critics and box-office. In his *Daily Record* letter, Corrie cited *The Ancient Fire* as an example of the Players' 'difficulty in discrimi-nating literature from drama'. In charging the Players with anti-socialist bias, therefore, he was not simply accusing them of political motivation but was ques-tioning their ability to take *any* kind of informed decision regarding the plays that the company produced.

The Players, not unnaturally, were enraged by this suggestion. Glen McKemmie, Convenor of the Board, wrote to the paper, abusing Corrie for his ingratitude to the Players and justifying both the decision to reject *In Time o' Strife* and stage *The Ancient Fire*. David Cleghorn Thomson, in a more reason-able letter, took much the same approach, taking Corrie to task for 'crabbing *The Ancient Fire*'. Significantly, however, both replies ignored the central charge of Corrie's argument: that the Reading Committee was ill-equipped for the job they were supposed to be doing. A glance at the composition of that committee will soon demonstrate the validity of this charge—at least, as far as the rejection of *In Time o' Strife* is concerned.

The three members of the Reading Committee were all writers whose interest in drama was primarily of a literary nature. The senior, undoubtedly most influential member was the aforementioned John Brandane. Brandane (real name MacIntyre) was a Glasgow doctor whose interest in play-writing had been stimulated by the example of the Abbey Theatre. As such, he was profoundly suspicious of any departure from the Abbey's example; although he had no choice but to welcome Guthrie's success, he never entirely approved of it. Corrie's naturalism probably scared Brandane more than his politics did.

The youngest, probably least influential, member of the committee was William Jeffrey, a journalist who was at that time a leader-writer for the *Glasgow Herald*. As the son of a colliery manager in Wishaw, Jeffrey may well have been out of sympathy with Corrie's view of the General Strike, but it is equally likely that his opposition to the play stemmed from quite another direction. Jeffrey was an accomplished poet who was deeply concerned with the re-emergence of Scots as a literary language. It is at least possible that Corrie's demotic dialect, which inevitably reflects the imperfections of actual speech, may have caused Jeffrey to take exception to the play on aesthetic grounds.

The last of the trio is by far the most intriguing. Like Brandane—who was very much his mentor at this time—Osborne Henry Mavor was a Glasgow doctor who adopted a pen-name to disguise his playwrighting activities from his patients. In the years ahead, James Bridie would exert an enormous influence on the development of theatre in Scotland. This influence will be given much fuller consideration in a later chapter, but at this point it should be noted that, in the person of Bridie, the canny Scots doctor was often at war with the adventurous playwright. As his son, Ronald Mavor, was to note in a memoir of his father which appeared 60 years later, Bridie's difficulties as a dramatist stemmed from a genuine moral dilemma.

> The sort of person he was, and the experiences which he had, made him distrustful of the Dionysiac side of his nature. The influence of the admirable Dr Mavor may not always have been good for Mr Bridie.

In 1927, it was certainly not good for Joe Corrie. Many years later, another Reading Committee, that of the Glasgow Citizens', would reject another Corrie play, *A Master of Men*. On that occasion, Bridie simply over-turned the decision and ordered that the play be put into production. As Chairman of the Citizens' board, he had the power to do this, but in the case of *In Time o' Strife*, he was not nearly so influential. Even if he had been, however, his innate sense of social conservatism would probably have affected his attitude to the play.

It is noticeable that the composition of the Reading Committee did not include an actor or anyone who had more than a passing acquaintance with the considerations of production. Much more important than the *presence* of political motives on that committee was the complete *absence* of any theatrical instinct. Tyrone Guthrie, who had of course been responsible for the successful production and tour of the earlier Corrie plays, does not appear to have been consulted on this matter. As for the members of the company—the actual Scottish National Players themselves—their views were probably the last to be taken into account.

Whatever these views may have been, however, the fact is that, once again, a Glasgow-based theatre company which had been brought into existence to create a genuinely Scottish theatre, had let a major opportunity pass it by. A production of *In Time o' Strife* by the Scottish National Players may have lacked the raw authenticity of the Fife Miners—and, as such, proved less successful—but it would certainly have carried the company nearer to its declared objective. As it was, the whole business revealed a serious flaw in the company's structure.

This went much further than simply the shortcomings of the Reading Committee. The root of the problem lay in a certain lack of dynamism, created by the company's amateur status. Theatrical instinct is created as a direct consequence of professional pressure—when one's livelihood is at stake, it concentrates the mind wonderfully—and, in the absence of such pressure, errors of omission are too easily made. In this respect, the experience of *The Ancient Fire* is more illuminating than that of *In Time o' Strife*.

Gunn's play is far from being an inconsequential work, although not, perhaps, its author's finest. (Recycled as *The Poaching at Grianan*, it was successfully published as a novella in 1930 and, 20 years later, would score a modest success at the Edinburgh Festival in a re-written version entitled *Beyond the Cage*.) Towards the end of his life, Neil Gunn told one of his biographers that he 'was trying to do a new sort of thing, trying to capture talk—talk in which people never say quite what they mean'. Whatever its imperfections, therefore, *The Ancient Fire* was a work of some substance and ambition, requiring the utmost degree of thought and preparation to be put in its productions. All the indications are that the play did not receive such careful preparation.

Tyrone Guthrie had, by this time, left the company. His father's recent death had created a family crisis which had obliged him to resign and return home. This, in turn, created a crisis in the affairs of the Scottish National Players. With no time to find a successor, Elliot Mason took over the direction of *The Ancient Fire*. Mason, a niece of the famous Misses Cranston of tea-shop fame, was a woman of independent means who would later become a successful actress in the West End and in films. At this time, however, she was still an amateur, a founder-member of the company who had been acting as Guthrie's assistant. There is some evidence to suggest that Elliot Mason's deficiencies as a director were at least partially to blame for the play's failure. Since Neil Gunn had been unable to attend the opening night, he had to rely on friends for news of the production. One of these, John Macnair Reid, was enthusiastic about the play, but told Gunn that 'the cast is very middling and the producing amateurish'.

Whatever the truth of the matter, it is quite clear that the Players had not grasped the crucial importance of this production. A new play by a talented Scottish author—precisely the kind of drama the company had been brought into being to create—should never have been permitted to take the stage without the best preparation possible. In the final analysis, one is forced to the conclusion that *The Ancient Fire* suffered, not from any lack of effort to secure its success, but from an inadequate concern regarding its failure. Unless such a concern could be instilled into the company, the Scottish National Players had gone about as far as they could go.

Brandane and Bridie, to be fair to them, were aware of the problem and tried to do something about it. In 1931, together with T J Honeyman—yet another Glasgow doctor!—they put forward a scheme to transform the Scottish National Players into a professional company. The idea was to take the Athenaeum Theatre for a professional season which would be guaranteed against loss by a number of influential backers whose support Bridie had managed to engage. It was a good idea—which Bridie would put into practice 12 years later with the Glasgow Citizens'– but the Scottish National Players wanted nothing to do with it.

The trouble was that most of the company had too much to lose. The idea might have appealed to such as Elliot Mason, a woman of independent means who would shortly make her professional debut in London, but most of the others had secure professional jobs that they did not wish to give up—at least, not at that time. In the years ahead, a number of the Players, such as James Gibson, Moultrie Kelsall and Jean Taylor-Smith, would enter the ranks of the acting profession, but the majority failed to see what Bridie saw—that the alternative to going professional would be fatal for the company's future.

On the rejection of the Athenaeum scheme, Bridie resigned from the board in disgust and the outcome was exactly as he had predicted. The Scottish National Players was wound up as a company in 1934, and although the Players remained in existence as an amateur club until 1947, the quality of their productions gradually diminished.

There is a degree of irony in the fact that Joe Corrie's company came to grief at much the same time. The Fife Miners, of course, were a professional company and, since they were earning 20 times more from acting than they had from their previous jobs, they would have been more than happy to remain professional. Unfortunately, a series of unrelated incidents led to the company's demise. Margaret McLean misbehaved herself once too often and was sacked, Benny Ogilvie the stage-manager was killed in a motor-cycle accident, Joe Corrie and George Ogilvie fell out over the non-payment of royalties and, finally, in 1931 Hugh Ogilvie died. With no-one to represent them, the Fife Miner Players had no choice but to give up the road and return home.

As for Corrie himself, he remained committed to his principles for the rest of his days. From 1932 on, he increasingly became involved with the Scottish Community Drama Association (SCDA), writing plays for companies like the Glasgow Corporation Transport Players, the Shotts Miner's Welfare Drama Group and the Newbattle Burns Dramatic Society, for whom he wrote one of the finest of all his one-acters, *Hewers of Coal*. He supported himself completely by his writing; in addition to his plays, he wrote stories and articles for newspapers, magazines, radio, trying everything, in his own words, 'where there was a guinea or two to be earned'. A novel, *Black Earth*, was published in 1939 and his drama was to have two more outings on the professional stage: *A Master of Men* (1944) and *The Roving Boy* (1958), both produced by Glasgow Citizens' Theatre.

His political values, too, remained intact, despite suggestions to the contrary. In the aftermath of the General Strike, a new working-class theatre movement began to gather strength. The Workers' Theatre Movement (WTM) believed that the prime function of theatre was a political one, and their centre of operations was not the village hall or the Variety theatre, but the picket line and street demonstration. (On 1 May, 1932, for instance, four members of the Dundee WTM were arrested for performing at a socialist rally.) By a curious irony, while this form of direct action effected no political change whatsoever, it developed performance techniques—street theatre, living newspaper etc.—which have since been absorbed into mainstream theatre.

The most important product of the Workers' Theatre Movement was Glasgow Unity, which began operations in 1940 with a production of Clifford Odets' *Awake and Sing*. Formed as a result of the fusion of a number of left-wing amateur companies, including the Clarion Players, the Glasgow Transport Players and Avrom Greenbaum's company at the Jewish Institute, Glasgow Unity became a focus of cultural activity during the dark days of the Second World War. Its political stance was primarily anti-fascist, with a play policy that showed a predilection for Russian and American Drama. While Unity's operations were initially confined to Glasgow, the 1945 production of Gorky's *The Lower Depths* transferred to the Westminster Theatre in London, and it was at about this time that a number of its members—including such as Russell Hunter, Ida Schuster, Roddy McMillan and Andrew Keir—turned professional.

Glasgow Unity, however, was only indirectly connected with the Workers' Theatre Movement, which was, in the main, severely critical of Joe Corrie. This was partly because of his association with the SCDA (which they regarded as a right-wing organisation) and partly because of the lack of overt political content in many of his plays. To criticise Corrie on such grounds, however, is to profoundly misunderstand the nature of both the man and his work.

In 1932, Corrie wrote an article for the *Scottish Stage* which is, in this respect, most revealing. After naming Ibsen, O'Neill and O'Casey as his favourite playwrights, he declared himself a little disillusioned with them and went on to say

What we want now from our dramatists is hope. But so long have we been accustomed to this hopelessness of dramatic tragedy that it is going to be difficult, for, as the old saying goes 'As the old cock crows, the young one learns.' The young dramatists have followed in the footsteps of the old.

Take any of the real serious plays of today. In how many of them do you get the stirring trumpet call that man will yet be a god? Cannot the tragedy of life be shown, not to show us how hopeless a proposition Man is, but to show us that only by conquering—not lying down to—life's difficulties and sorrows can we emerge to something greater?

How often do we get the evil that is in Man without any hint as to the cause. And are we not all moulded so much by our environment and our circumstances that there is a cause for almost every evil and folly we are heir to? Sean O'Casey had a great opportunity and failed; he had no hope at all for his working comrades.

It may seem odd to describe Sean O'Casey as a failure—and only Joe Corrie could make such a statement so unequivocally!—but, when one considers the nature of Corrie's aspirations, this opinion is entirely justified. It is certainly true that O'Casey's powers as a playwright waned when he became separated from his roots.

All his life, Corrie remained committed to the scene that was described at the beginning of this chapter; he would sooner have no theatrical success at all than fail in this context. During the 'hungry thirties', when his people were suffering as never before, his object was not to tell them why they were suffering—they were all only too aware of that—but to write plays for them to perform and enjoy, plays that would allow them to believe in themselves, would give them hope. As one of the Fife Miners, William 'Misty' Thomson said of him: 'Joe, he was more than a gentleman—he was a working-class man. Everybody in his own area was a brother, every woman was a sister. The higher-ups were nothing to him, he wasn't interested in them.'

Even so, Joe Corrie's work was to have a lasting influence, going far beyond his time and place and class. In the Scottish Theatre today, this influence is writ very large indeed, not only in terms of his plays—many of which are as viable today as they were when they were written—but in terms of his whole theatrical approach. In the great upsurge of Scottish dramatic writing that began 30 years ago and continues apace, the marks of this influence can be clearly seen. Simplicity of form, directness of statement, commitment to community and, most of all, a profound concern with social justice, are prominent characteristics of contemporary Scottish drama at its best—and all of these qualities have been inherited from Joe Corrie.

Less directly, perhaps, this influence was also felt in performance. The many plays that Corrie and others wrote for the SCDA inevitably led to the evolution of a distinctive acting style. Among the thousands of actors who contributed to this evolution were many whose talent and ambition felt frustrated by their amateur status. For such actors—the pioneers of the re-emerging Scottish acting profession—the problem that Bridie had identified in the Scottish National Players loomed increasingly large. There is little point in having professional ambitions if there is no professional theatre in which to put them into practice.

As things turned out, this problem would be solved with the aid of a most unlikely ally. In the early '30s, a professional company arrived in Scotland to play repertory seasons in Edinburgh and Glasgow. In time, this company—which was wholly English in both composition and repertoire—would be led by an English actor-manager who would make Scotland his home and, over the years, transform the company into a veritable Scottish national institution.

Chapter Nine

WILSON BARRETT AND THE PROFESSIONALS

The period of the London actor-managers lasted for approximately 50 years. During this time (as noted earlier) the British Theatre was unified as never before; performances given in Scotland by such as Henry Irving, John Laurence Toole, Edward Compton, Charles Wyndham, George Alexander and others differed little, if at all, from their performances in London. In those days, the difference between 'West End' and 'Provinces' was merely geographical, and playgoers in Edinburgh, Glasgow, Aberdeen etc. had no sense of having an inferior theatrical experience from that which could be enjoyed in London. It was a genuine unity, capable of accommodating every strand of British culture—but it came to an end in August 1914, with the outbreak of the First World War.

This war changed everything in British society, bringing about cataclysmic changes in the quality of daily life. In the theatre, however, its immediate effect was to create a boom in business, as people turned in their droves to the theatre in a desperate desire for escapism. This boom attracted large-scale investment and, while seat prices were maintained at pre-war level, theatre rents rose at an alarming rate. In 1914 the average theatre rent was £25 per week; by 1920, this figure had risen to £500. The actor-managers, who had always operated on narrow margins, could not possibly afford to absorb such costs, and most of them either went out of business or threw in their lot with the new production companies that came into being at that time.

There was more to this, however, than simply economics. After four years of the most terrible hardships, it was found that public taste had undergone something of a sea-change. Musical comedy enjoyed perhaps its greatest popularity at this time, with its bright lights, its catchy tunes, its daring chorus girls and its exciting matinee idols. The horrors of war and the sense of relief at its passing induced a fashion for the flippant and the superficial. This led to the 'Roaring Twenties', the decade of the Charleston and the flapper, the 'It Girl' and 'Anything Goes'. It was a time in which people desperately needed to be 'taken out of themselves', that they might forget both their memories of the immediate past and their apprehensions concerning the expected future.

As far as legitimate drama was concerned, this change in taste led to a profound change in the nature of performance. Cedric Hardwicke, who began his career before the War as a member of Frank Benson's company and returned to the stage with Barry Jackson at the Birmingham Rep in 1922, noticed this change immediately. In his autobiography, *Let's Pretend* (Grayson & Grayson, 1932), he describes the situation most succinctly.

> Acting was entering on a new phase where 'Let's pretend' had given way to 'Let's be.' The realism of the cinema which, far away in Hollywood, had been entirely untouched by the European imbroglio, had made vast strides and had trained audiences to demand less theatre and more life. A more subtle technique had been created, and although the basic principles of making oneself seen and heard remained the same, these ends had now to be reached by less obvious methods.

This change in the perceptions of the audience, together with the new economic conditions, led to the demise of the actor-manager companies. In Scotland, this created something of a problem for the theatrical establishment, then in the hands of the Edinburgh-based Howard & Wyndham Ltd.

This company, which had been created out of the partnership between J B Howard and Robert Wyndham's son, Fred, had been established in 1895, at which time it owned four theatres. Twenty years later, this number had risen to ten and throughout the '20s the company's fortunes continued to rise until, by the time of Fred Wyndham's death in 1930, there was scarcely a theatre in the United Kingdom in which Howard & Wyndham did not have an interest. Most of these theatres could, in one way or another, adapt to the new conditions and the problem only arose in certain select houses—the Royal Lyceum in Edinburgh and the Theatre Royal, Glasgow—where there was a tradition of serious drama.

The actor-managers were replaced, in the first instance, by production companies run by investors whose main objective was to make as much profit as possible. To this end, they would seek to maximise profits on a West End success by sending a duplicate company on tour. This was a policy which, for all its economic sense, often proved to be self-defeating. For instance, in 1926, one of the hits of the London season was a play by Michael Arlen called *The Green Hat*. This success had been the exclusive creation of the starring rôle, which was played by Tallulah Bankhead. When *The Green Hat* toured Scotland, however, Miss Bankhead did not appear—her place was taken by a lesser-known actress called Phyllis Thomas—and this not only robbed the play of its appeal but created a negative impression in the theatres that featured in the tour. Audiences who had previously been accustomed to the best that London could offer were now being told that they would have to settle for second-best. Not surprisingly, business suffered.

Howard & Wyndham sought to remedy the situation by recourse to the

Repertory Movement. In doing so—although no-one realised this at the time—
they were taking the first steps in re-constituting the Scottish Stage. For the first
time in decades, Scottish theatres began to acquire resident companies.

At first sight, the Repertory system seems to bear a close resemblance to the
old Stock system, in that Rep companies are contracted to perform a season of
plays in a particular place. There is, however, one crucial difference. Repertory
actors, unlike Stock actors, were not required for specific 'lines of business', but
quite the contrary. In Weekly Rep, every actor had to keep three quite separate
parts in mind; the part that was rehearsed during the day, the part that was
played at night, and the part that was in preparation for rehearsal on the following week. Since these parts varied considerably in length and difficulty—this
week's leading rôle could be next week's walk-on and vice versa—each actor
needed to be extremely versatile, revealing what was perhaps the most crucial
difference between the old system and the new. In Stock, the cast was chosen to
fit the plays: in Repertory, the plays were chosen to fit the cast.

Although the work of the repertory actor was, of course, extremely demand-
ing, there was a positive, creative and, indeed, enjoyable side to it. In displaying
their versatility, week after week, to what was essentially the same audience, the
Rep companies developed an almost symbiotic relationship with their supporters. Actors attained a degree of local celebrity that was simply not available to
the touring companies and, what was more important, inevitably developed an
intimate awareness of the tastes and perceptions of their particular audience. As
a direct result of this, the Repertory companies gradually evolved their own
distinct identity.

Time was a important factor in this respect. No company, no matter how
talented, could expect instantaneous success and so a degree of financial backing
was required, either from organisations or individuals. The first professional
Repertory company to settle in Scotland successfully was the Brandon Thomas
Seasons, who played a six-week season at the Royal Lyceum, Edinburgh, in 1930.
Howard & Wyndham were trying out a number of companies at that time—
among them the St Martin's Players and Robert Fenemore's Masque Theatre—
and the fact that the Brandon Thomas company were able to settle in Scotland
was a direct result of the backing they received from Howard & Wyndham. In
the autumn of 1933, for instance, they played three months at the Glasgow
Theatre Royal before they made any profit at all. As their founder, Jevan Brandon-
Thomas remarked at the time, 'Howard and Wyndham were patience itself'
and, in time, this patience was rewarded. After this inauspicious start, the Brandon
Thomas Seasons established a pattern which would continue, with one notable
intermission, for the next 20 years: summer residence in Edinburgh followed by
an autumn season in Glasgow.

In the beginning, the company was entirely English, both in composition
and outlook. Most of the actors came from London, or had been recruited there,
and the repertoire was dominated by the leading names in English drama at that
time: Coward, Maugham, Priestley, John Drinkwater and Frederick Lonsdale.

114

As they began to discover their audience, however, their work gradually assumed a Scottish dimension. The occasional Scottish actor was employed and new plays by Scottish playwrights, such as Donald Carswell and Robins Millar, were produced. As a matter of fact, their most important success—one of the greatest commercial successes that the Scottish Theatre has ever known—was achieved with a play that was based on a famous incident in Scottish history.

Margot Lister's *Swords about the Cross* tells the story of Mary, Queen of Scots, from her girlhood in France to her execution in England. Produced by Brandon Thomas in 1936, it was a hugely expensive affair, involving a cast of 33 featured rôles, plus an equivalent number of supers, with incidental music provided by the celebrated Dolmetsch Orchestra. This expense was more than amply justified by the fact that the production broke all box-office records, being seen by an amazing 42,000 people in a period of two weeks. The part of Mary was played by a pretty young actress from the Old Vic called Nancy Hornsby, Bothwell by Jevan Brandon-Thomas himself, and the central rôle of Darnley by his closest associate and eventual successor, Wilson Barrett.

At this time, Barrett was 36 years old and had been playing substantial rôles for the past ten years. Since he was the grandson of the famous Victorian actor-manager and dramatist whose name he bore, it is hardly surprising that theatre was in his blood. In later years, when asked about his hobbies, he would usually offer 'philately and golf' but his interest in such pastimes can only have been of a transitory nature. He was a man who lived for his work and his every waking moment was devoted to it.

The story of how Wilson Barrett took over from Jevan Brandon-Thomas is slightly complicated and a little unpleasant. In 1937, rumours began to circulate concerning a homosexual love affair between Jevan Brandon-Thomas and a young Scottish actor from Perth, Alex MacAlpine. Whether or not these rumours had any foundation in fact was beside the point as far as A Stewart Cruikshank, managing director of Howard & Wyndham, was concerned. Gay relationships have never—to say the least—been uncommon in the theatre, but the attitude of most people at that time was very much as stated in the famous remark of Mrs Patrick Campbell: 'I don't care how these gentle people make love, as long as they don't do it in the street and scare the horses'. In Cruikshank's eyes, Brandon-Thomas had been scaring the horses and had to go. In a somewhat unceremonious manner, the Brandon Thomas Seasons were evicted from the Scottish theatres where they had been so successful.

Wilson Barrett was untouched by this scandal. By this time, he had left the company and was acting at the Arts Theatre in London. In 1938, however, he was approached by a financial backer—whose identity has never been revealed—with a surprising and completely unexpected offer. After his eviction from Scotland, Jevan Brandon-Thomas had tried to continue in business by taking two suburban London theatres; the King's, Hammersmith, and the Wimbledon Theatre. He had been promised financial backing for this venture but, for some mysterious reason, it had been withdrawn. Brandon-Thomas was now bankrupt and all his actors were out of work. Barrett was assured that, if he agreed to take over the company, financial backing would be provided.

After initial hesitation—although he was experienced in acting and production, he knew nothing about the administrative side of theatre—Barrett decided to take the plunge, in partnership with Esmond Knight, a well-known West End actor at the time. The members of the former Brandon Thomas Seasons were immediately contacted and, on 24 January, 1939, 'Wilson Barrett and Esmond Knight Ltd.' opened at the King's Theatre, Hammersmith, with Noël Coward's triple bill, *Tonight at 8.30.*

At this point, it should be understood that a permanent return to Scotland was never part of Barrett's plans. Although they were prepared to play summer seasons in Edinburgh and Glasgow, the idea from the first was to make Hammersmith their base. As Barrett records in his account of the company, *On Stage for Notes* (Blackwood, 1954), the King's was perfect for their purpose, in that 'it was far enough from the West End to avoid competition with the star attractions there, and not far enough to discourage managers from coming to see new plays and players'. The eventual return to Scotland came about purely as a result of the chaotic conditions that prevailed at the time.

In the summer of 1939, the company played a season of nine weeks at the Empire, Edinburgh. On the day after this season ended, 3 September, war was declared and all theatres were immediately closed. This embargo remained in force for some time in London, so it was impossible for the company to return to Hammersmith as originally planned. When Barrett was offered a further six weeks at the Empire, he accepted gratefully. Although this season played to disastrous business—in these first few weeks of war, nobody wanted to go to the theatre—Moss Empires engaged the company for a five-week tour, which included the Glasgow Alhambra. By this time, business had improved enormously, every house was sold out and they were given a rapturous reception. As a result of this, they were offered a contract of 12 summer weeks for the next two years.

After this Glasgow success, the company returned to London, where theatres were beginning to re-open. The 1939 season at the King's was better than expected, but in 1940 there was no business at all. In an attempt to find a home for the company, Barrett returned to Edinburgh to explore his Scottish contacts and, while there, was offered some radio work in Bristol. On his return journey from this trip, just north of Gretna, Barrett's train was involved in a head-on collision with another.

Barrett had a seat very near to the front of the train. He was thrown the complete length of the carriage and, although he does not seem to have lost consciousness at any time, landed very badly on the small of his back. Once he had gathered his wits, he found he could not move and lay for several hours while firemen, ambulancemen etc. extracted the casualties. After eight days in a local infirmary, he found that his mobility had returned, albeit with a great deal of pain. What followed is the clearest indication of the tremendous reserve of inner strength that Wilson Barrett possessed.

Determined to continue with his business, Barrett dressed himself with difficulty, discharged himself from hospital, hired a car and drove to Edinburgh, where he had been lodging at the home of a Scottish actor called Neil Crawford. When Crawford's mother saw how badly injured Barrett was, she immediately sent for her doctor, who ordered an X-ray. As a result of this examination, it was revealed that Barrett's spine had been crushed, his pelvis fractured in two places and the socket in his thigh-bone split right across. He was to spend the next three months in Edinburgh, encased in plaster.

It must have been a frustrating and depressing time for him. In London, where the Blitz was at its worst, the company was doing practically no business at all and the only bright spot on the horizon was the summer booking at the Glasgow Alhambra. (As Barrett later admitted, it was only the thought of this booking that kept the company going.) On the other hand, it is probable that this enforced rest had a beneficial effect, in that it allowed him to recuperate from two years of considerable mental and physical strain. By the time the company opened at the Alhambra in May 1941, he was almost back to normal. After a slow start, the Glasgow season began to show a profit and, by the seventh week, the company had received an offer of a season at the Royal Lyceum in Edinburgh. From then on, the company was based in Scotland.

It is at this point in the company's history that the Scottish dimension begins to assume significance. Although business was good, their problems were far from over, and one of the most pressing of these was a serious shortage of personnel. With so many young men—and not a few young women—disappearing into the forces, there was a continual difficulty in casting the plays. Although Barrett was later to remark, in a joking manner, that he was reduced to considering 'hunchbacks, schoolboys and elderly gentlemen of between sixty and eighty', the truth is that he largely solved this difficulty by resort to the Scottish amateur theatre. The merest glance at the company's records will show that a number of Scottish amateurs—Jamieson Clark, Brown Derby, James Gibson, Eileen Herlie, Elizabeth Sellars and Pat Sandys—gained valuable professional experience at this time.

The contribution that such actors made undoubtedly enabled the Wilson Barrett company to survive the war. They also played a substantial part in the considerable success that Barrett enjoyed in the immediate post-war decade. Walter Carr, Archie Duncan, Robert James, Lennox Milne, Bryden Murdoch, Edith MacArthur, Grace McChlery, Robert Urquhart, John Young and many other names that would become instantly familiar to Scottish playgoers were very much part of the company at this time. Although the company was never exclusively Scottish—and, in fact, always retained the middle-class, middle-brow, essentially London-centred orientation it had had from the beginning—a definite change began to take place in the character of its performances with the passing of the years.

At the height of its success, the activities of the Wilson Barrett company followed a distinct pattern. The first season of the year would take place in

Wilson Barrett's last appearance in Edinburgh, in Moray Maclaren's *Heather on Fire*

Edinburgh from February until May, after which they would move to Glasgow until September, when they would return to Edinburgh until Christmas. At the end of 1947, a short season in Aberdeen was included in the itinerary and, from then on, the company played regular seasons in all three cities.

For Wilson Barrett personally, the inclusion of the Aberdeen season was a great delight. Apart from the fact that he had a particular fondness for the city and its people, Aberdeen had a certain romantic association with his family history. It was while playing at the Aberdeen Theatre Royal under McNeill's management in 1869 that his grandfather had fallen in love with his grandmother, Caroline Heath. After a whirlwind courtship, they had been married at the end of their engagement and had returned to the city many times, both socially and professionally. In 1948, in fact, Barrett was taken aback by one aged playgoer who told him that he'd hardly changed since *The Sign of the Cross*! Although it amused him to be associated with his grandfather's greatest hit, he must have been agreeably surprised to find that his name was still remembered in the city after so many years.

By the early '50s, the name of Wilson Barrett had become synonymous with the best that theatre in Scotland had to offer. More than 30 plays were put into production annually during these years, and the seasons at Edinburgh, Glasgow and Aberdeen consistently drew enthusiastic support. (This achievement is all the more remarkable when one considers that the company received neither sponsorship or public subsidy of any kind, its survival depending wholly on box-office revenue. At the time of Barrett's accident, his anonymous financial backer, fearful of the future, had withdrawn his support and Barrett had been obliged to sell everything he owned in order to fulfil his obligations to the Glasgow Alhambra in 1941.) Successful as they were, however, they were not the only repertory company in the field.

In the early months of 1935, two young actors were waiting for a train to take them back to London from Ilford, where they had been playing with the Lena Ashwell Players. Their names were David Steuart and Marjorie Dence and they were old friends, having first met while members of London University Dramatic Society. On the wall of the station waiting room, there was a map of Scotland and, in the course of a casual conversation, Steuart pointed to the town of Perth and expressed an ambition to open a repertory theatre there. A few days later, Dence was at breakfast with her family when she happened to notice an advert in the *Stage* newspaper, announcing that there was a theatre for sale in Perth. She mentioned this coincidence to her father in a fairly casual manner and, to her complete astonishment, was told that if she and Steuart thought they could make a go of such a venture, Mr Dence would make enquiries with a view to buying the building.

The building that Mr Dence bought was not the old Perth Theatre Royal that Corbet Ryder had helped to establish in 1820—that had become a clothing factory in 1845—but the theatre in the High Street which is still in use today, erected by a consortium of civic-minded Perth businessmen in 1899. On 23 September, 1935, it became the home of Perth Repertory Theatre.

A glance at the early records of Perth Rep reveals a company of much the same kind as that of Wilson Barrett. It was, in short, another English company which had settled in Scotland, employing the same kind of actors to perform the same kind of plays. The only real difference lay in the fact that the potential audience of Perth was very much smaller than that of Edinburgh or Glasgow and, as result, Perth Rep had a greater struggle to become established. With the outbreak of war, this struggle became even harder, forcing many to the conclusion that Perth Rep could not possibly survive.

In fact, the story of Perth Rep's survival through the early days of the Second World War is one of the most heroic episodes in the entire history of Scottish Theatre. On 3 September, 1939, when the Government ordered all the theatres to close, Perth's resources were so low that the entire company had to be paid off. Just as this was being arranged, news came through that the theatres were going to be allowed to open again very shortly. It was at this point that someone, most probably Marjorie Dence herself, came up with a plan to keep the theatre open on a share-out basis. The actors moved into the theatre—sleeping in the dressing-rooms, coffee-bar and so on—and took over all the non-playing functions: box office, cleaning, scene shifting etc. Volunteers turned up to sell programmes and serve refreshments. At the end of each week, after dealing with all necessary expenses, what remained of the takings was shared out. In 1956, on the occasion of the company's 21st birthday, Marjorie Dence recalled this period.

A gypsy sort of life it was, but somehow there was a grand sense of comradeship. Just because the living conditions were so hard and the financial reward so negligible, we attracted only people with the right spirit, who were keen on the work for its own sake. We also felt that we were doing something to save our beloved theatre from extinction, besides bringing some brightness to the lives of our audiences at a time when it was badly needed.

This contribution to the war effort did not pass without notice or reward. In 1941, when the Council for the Encouragement of Music and the Arts (CEMA as it was known) came into being, the company was given financial assistance on condition that it undertook a fairly rigorous touring schedule. Over the next five years, in addition to its regular season, Perth Rep toured far and wide: to the Highlands, the Outer Hebrides, Orkney and Shetland, the Borders and, on two occasions, Northern Ireland. In 1946, in a quite unprecedented move, Perth and Kinross County Council formed a committee of management to run the theatre company, employing David Steuart and Marjorie Dence as Artistic Director and Business Manager respectively. With CEMA matching the local authorities support with annual grants, Perth Repertory Theatre was placed on a sound financial basis.

This development is indicative of a complete change of attitude that was taking place in Scottish life. The idea of 'civic theatre' was in the air and gathered momentum in the post-war period of reconstruction. For the first time in history, theatre was seen as having a function that served the common good: no longer simply a social pastime, but an art form that was capable of being put to social and economic use. Besides being a useful tool in the growing new industry of tourism, the presence of a theatre company, it was thought, would enhance the quality of life in any given community.

The involvement of a Scottish local authority in theatrical affairs was to have wide-reaching consequences. In 1939, just four years after the foundation of Perth Rep, a touring manager called Robert Thornley arrived in the neighbouring city of Dundee. Thornley's company had played Dundee a few years earlier but the theatre they had taken on that occasion, the Alhambra, had since been converted into a cinema and there was nowhere for them to perform. The Dundee Dramatic Society, the city's leading amateur company, had however recently acquired new premises in a old jute store. Thornley approached this organisation with a plan to create a permanent repertory company in the city. This plan was accepted, the two companies came together, a suitable theatre was found in Nicoll Street and, in December 1939, Dundee Repertory Theatre was born.

Although the early years of Dundee Rep were full of as much difficulty as those of Perth Rep, there was the advantage of a much larger potential audience, who gave the company enthusiastic support from the beginning and cared enough about their local theatre to ensure it survived the difficult years. In addition to this, Dundee Rep had the benefit of the talents of two quite remarkable men; George Geddes and A R Whatmore. Geddes, a member of Dundee Dramatic Society, had been one of the first supporters of Robert Thornley's proposals and devoted the rest of his life to their successful implementation. A local business-man who was possessed of dynamic organisational skills and great personal mag-netism, Geddes brought a great deal of drive and energy to the administration of the company's affairs.

A R Whatmore was 53 years old when he took over as artistic director from Robert Thornley in 1942. He was a man of the widest experience, both as actor and manager. Prior to the First World War, he had toured the country with Lewis Waller's company and, throughout the '20s and '30s, had been kept in more or less continuous employment as an actor in the West End. He had also directed productions at most of the leading London theatres and, as early as 1923, had established a repertory company in Hull. In 1940, he made an unsuc-cessful attempt to found a similar company in Aberdeen. Dundee, however, was to be the crowning glory of his career. Over the next decade, he would trans-form Dundee Rep into one of the the most celebrated repertory companies in the land—and, even then, he wasn't satisfied. In 1952, at an age when most men would be contemplating retirement, he announced his ambition of winning an international reputation by taking the company on a world tour. 'All it would take' he told a meeting of the theatre's board 'is fifty thousand pounds and a spirit of adventure!'

Although this ambition was never to be fulfilled, a spirit of adventure has never been lacking in Scotland's repertory companies. Perth and Dundee have both had to come through some extremely hard times but are still in existence at the time of writing, as is another company which is even older. In 1933, some members of a Church Bible Class in St Andrews applied to the town council for the lease of a byre on a disused farm. Their object was to create a little theatre to act as a home for the amateur productions with which they had been competing in the SCDA play festivals. Originally the St Andrews Play Club, they eventu-ally became the Byre Theatre company.

Unlike the other companies mentioned in this chapter, the Byre developed naturally from within the community and not through the ambitious efforts of any outsider. There was never any shortage of ambition, however. Fifty years later, the company's founder, A B Paterson, remembered the motivations of the early years in a pamphlet he wrote to commemorate the anniversary.

> Each summer the Play Club presented a repertoire of plays for the entertainment of visitors and residents. Eager to improve our technical knowledge, the club used the money made in the summer to finance one of the members, Russell Mather, to attend as a full-time student the two years' course at the Edinburgh Drama College from 1937-39, on the understanding that at weekends he passed on to the members what he had learned during the week.

As a result of such dedicated enthusiasm, it was clear that the company could not be contained by the Amateur Movement. In 1940, Elliot Playfair, an actor from St Andrews who was a member of the Perth company, arrived with a company to present the first professional season. Playfair was assisted by

Charles Marford, formerly of the Old Vic, and it was Marford and his wife, Molly Tapper, who kept the company going during the difficult war years. When Paterson returned from the forces in 1945, he re-assumed the running of the theatre, but it was not until 1947 that the Byre established its own unique system of production.

The amateurs occupied the theatre during the winter months, employing each year a professional producer, who would form his or her own company to run a season of plays from April until December. This system remained in place until 1969, when the company moved into its present building and the production pattern adopted a similar system to the other reps. As was the case with Perth and Dundee, the Byre formed an association with the local authority and CEMA (which later became the Scottish Arts Council) and enjoyed its most fruitful period in the early '50s.

When one considers the success of such companies—and two others, to be discussed in the next chapter—it is clear that the immediate post-war decade represents something of a golden age for the theatre in Scotland. What with Wilson Barrett in Edinburgh, Glasgow and Aberdeen, Steuart and Dence in Perth, Whatmore in Dundee and Paterson in St Andrews, the professional theatre in Scotland was in a healthier state than it had been for almost a century. Despite all this success, however, there was one fly in the ointment, a fatal flaw that would undermine so much valuable work. For all their dedicated devotion to their respective communities, these companies were not perceived as being truly Scottish, but as alien imports. Even the Byre, with its roots in the oldest university town in Scotland, was regarded by many as an outpost of provincial English rep.

In many ways, of course, this charge seems outrageously unfair. It ignores the significance of these developments and completely misunderstands the organic nature of theatre. As we have seen, Wilson Barrett brought many Scottish actors into his company and this is true of Perth, Dundee and St Andrews as well. Not only did these companies provide training for novices, they enabled older Scottish actors—such as John Laurie and Sophie Stewart—who had been obliged to find such training in London, to work once more in their native land. Playwrights, too, were to benefit: Barrie, Bridie, Graham Moffat and Aimee Stuart found a regular place in the repertoire, while younger writers, such as Alexander Reid, Donald McLaren and A B Paterson himself received their first opportunities. Wilson Barrett was particularly encouraging in this respect and even made a fairly successful attempt to revive the Waverley Dramas, when he commissioned a new adaptation of *The Heart of Midlothian* from Clarke Claypole. All in all, it would appear that the Scottish reps did as much for Scottish Drama as they possibly could.

In addition to this, it should be remembered that, in those days, the Scottish identity was largely subsumed in a wider identity, created by the British Empire. Although the cracks in the structure of this Empire grew increasingly wider from 1945 on, much of its legacy remained in place. The terms Scottish, Scotch,

Scots etc. were often used in a pejorative sense, as signifying something slightly inferior, certainly vulgar. In the schools, children would be reprimanded for committing a 'scotticism' in an essay, and chastised (often physically) if they as much as uttered a Scots word in the classroom. Educated Scots, including actors—although not, it must be admitted, the best of them—took great pains to disguise their origins, even while remaining in Scotland. A Received English accent was the first acquisition that Scottish students were expected to make on entering university, and any interest that was taken in Scottish literature, language or history was regarded as quaint. As a matter of fact, ignorance of such subjects was acknowledged as an essential sign of sophistication and good taste. Any sense of Scottish identity, in short, was equated with disadvantage.

Bearing this in mind, the remarkable thing about the Scottish reps was not their essentially English outlook—given the background of most of their founders, this could hardly have been otherwise—but the fact that they acquired Scottish characteristics so quickly. The importance of such as Barrett, Steuart, Dence, Whatmore and Paterson is that their efforts aided the re-birth of the Scottish Theatre. If they did not create a new theatrical identity themselves, they at least sowed the seeds. As we have seen in previous chapters, there was no shortage of indigenous dramatic activity at this time and the example of the Repertory Movement in Scotland was a very inspiring one. These companies created, not simply theatrical centres for their respective communities, but an organisational framework in which Scottish Drama would eventually flourish. Given time—the essential element in repertory development—there is little doubt that the point would have been reached where the charge of provincialism would have become completely redundant.

These reservations apart, however, the charge retains a measure of validity—on artistic grounds, if no other. The problem was not a matter of any lack of *Scottish* identity, but rather one of any clear and definable *theatrical* identity. This was what lay at the heart of the failure of these companies to exploit and develop, in any meaningful way, the new dramatic impulse which, as we have seen, was emerging in Scotland at this time. Content to follow London in terms of production and performance, these companies were totally incapable of breaking free from London influence in terms of repertoire.

In 1929, a young Glasgow amateur, writing in the *Scottish Stage*, summed up the problem in a few short sentences.

> Dramatists, so dogmatic about the primary importance of the text, are failing consistently to realize a satisfactory form. May not this be due to the lack of a conscious and progressive system of acting, designed to merge finally with the words of the author in a Scottish Art of the Theatre?
> The Art of the Theatre is the art of conceiving a play as acted in a particular style in a particular place. Without this approach Scottish Drama will continue to waver indeterminately following the lead of the West End in a vicious Piccadilly Circus.

Over the next two decades, the Scottish Theatre was to make a successful effort to break out of this circle, aided in no small measure by the young actor who wrote these words and whose talent would inspire a whole generation. His name was Duncan Macrae.

Chapter Ten

RENAISSANCE—THE GREAT MACRAE

The story of Duncan Macrae must be seen in the context of the Scottish Renaissance, a cultural campaign which was born in the aftermath of the First World War with the object of re-invigorating the Scottish sense of identity. From the smallest of beginnings, the Scottish Renaissance was to have far-reaching effects on many aspects of Scottish life.

Among the survivors of 1918 was a young Scottish journalist called Christopher Murray Grieve, who was later to write that he 'came back with an *idée fixe*—never again must men be made to suffer as in these years of war'. This thought led to the development of a wider, even more deeply held conviction: that it was essential for the progress of humanity that the conventions of society be subjected to a rigorous and perpetual examination. If this seems a daunting task, Grieve's energies and intellect were equal to it. For the next 60 years, he never so much as wavered in his unreserved acceptance of Thomas Hardy's definition of literature as 'the written expression of revolt against accepted things.' In Grieve's case, this revolt took the form of poetry. Under the pseudonym of Hugh MacDiarmid (which he adopted in 1921), he was to write one of the greatest extended poems of the twentieth century: *A Drunk Man Looks at the Thistle*.

Although he was never popular—popularity was a concept that he affected to despise—Grieve was to become a highly influential figure in Scottish affairs—so much so, in fact, that it is often suggested that the Scottish Renaissance was his own single-handed creation. This is very far from being true, of course; the spirit of renewal which was abroad at this time was a spontaneous development and could never have been brought about by a single writer. Grieve was, however, its most eloquent spokesman and, in this respect, his poetry is of less importance than the fact that he was a trained journalist, skilled in the mechanics of publicity. Throughout the 1920s, from his base in Montrose, Grieve wrote a stream of articles, pamphlets, letters to the editor etc., attacking all and sundry, stirring up controversy at every conceivable opportunity. The motivation that lay behind this strategy was explained quite clearly in his book, *Contemporary Scottish Studies* (1926).

> The promoters of the Scottish Renaissance have all along realised that their ends could be achieved best by attracting some of their compatriots and antagonising others...they believe that in the balancing of these opposite effects will be achieved the all-round national awakening which is their objective.

The key word here is 'awakening'. The Scottish sense of identity had been asleep for far too long and it was Grieve's intention to wake it up. In doing so, however, he could not afford to mince his words or to express opinions which might in any way be construed as reasonable. He had to go continually for extremes: extremes of praise and extremes of condemnation. As far as his condemnation was concerned, however, his aim was not—at least, not usually—to obliterate his opponents, but to draw from them a stronger, more considered, response which would effectively raise the level of the argument, to the general benefit of Scottish artistic and intellectual life. He chose his targets and attacked them with a force that was almost brutal. In 1926, in that same book, he turned his attention to the Scottish National Players.

> It is at once pitiful and amusing to read that this precious society is determined to prove that there is a distinct Scottish drama on the strength of such plays as Mr Neil Grant's. A Scottish drama cannot be created in this way. This so-called 'movement' is doomed by shallowness of purpose, the absence of research, conscience, imaginative integrity and the mistake of thinking that it is possible to secure a Scottish drama as a mere offshoot of the contemporary English stage in its most ephemeral and trivial aspects; a freak of hybridisation, resembling the stoneless plum, is all that can be so secured.

Every condemnation, however, was balanced by an accompanying, equally uncompromising, expression of praise. In this case, Grieve's real object in attacking the Scottish National Players was to justify his approval of someone he very much admired and wished to encourage—R F Pollock.

Pollock, a Glasgow estate agent, was one of a number of amateur producers who were active at that time. Born in the Vale of Leven in 1885, he had been fascinated by theatre from an early age and, in later life, he would often recall the toy theatre he had as a child. While still in his teens, he had formed an amateur drama group among his friends and he maintained a serious interest in theatre for the rest of his life. His views were very much in accord with those of the Scottish Renaissance and, as such, very different from those of the Scottish National Players, although he appears to have remained on equable terms with the company. Indeed, it was in association with D Glen McKemmie, a former Chairman of the Players, that Pollock established the experimental Tron Theatre Club, based in the Keir Hardie Institute in Glasgow's Renfrew Street.

Although he was active for less than a decade—from the mid-1920s until his death in 1938—Pollock's influence on Scottish acting was to prove to be as important as Grieve's was on Scottish poetry. In 1926, during a visit to London, he had been excited by Theodor Komisjarevsky's Chekhov Season at the Barnes Repertory and had immediately become converted to the ideas that were being developed in the Soviet Theatre at that time. Later in the same year, he paid a visit to Moscow and had the pleasure of seeing these methods in action.

> Most people in the theatre are unwilling to understand that accident is not art, you cannot build on it. The master performer must have complete control of his instrument, and that of an artist is a complex mechanism. We actors have to deal not just with a voice the way a singer does, not just with hands like a pianist, not just with the body and legs like a dancer. We are obliged to play simultaneously on all the spiritual and physical aspects of a human being. To gain mastery over them requires time and arduous, systematic effort.

While Pollock could not have read the above quotation—it comes from *Building a Character* by Konstantin Stanislavsky, which was not published until 1949—it represents very much the kind of ideas that were interesting him at that time, and the Tron Theatre was formed with the intention of putting such ideas into practice. (In passing, it is interesting to note that two decades before Elia Kazan established the celebrated Actor's Studio in New York, Pollock was exploring Stanislavsky's ideas with a group of amateur actors in Glasgow.) Pollock's methods involved a very long rehearsal process of up to three months, a detailed analysis of every character, and an approach to staging that was almost automated in its precision. Every actor received a script which contained copious notes on every speech and exact instructions on every pause. In addition to this, Pollock would often write to his actors individually, spelling out his thoughts on the character in even greater detail.

It was an approach which was light years away from weekly rep and, as such, would have been completely impractical in the professional theatre. Requiring actors who possessed a degree of natural talent and dedication to his ideals, Pollock drew on the ranks of the Glasgow amateurs. He formed a company which included many who would later make an important mark on the professional stage: Eileen Herlie, Andrew Crawford, Molly Urquhart, Grace Ballantine and Paul Vincent Carroll. Most important of all Pollock's recruits, however, was a very tall, gaunt and gangling young man who was then employed as a primary school teacher: John Duncan Grahame Macrae.

Macrae was born in 1905, the fifth son of a Glasgow policeman who hailed originally from Sutherland. His father's successful police career—he was eventually promoted to the rank of Inspector in 1919—meant that Macrae had a comparatively prosperous and secure upbringing; he was educated at the fee-paying Allan Glen's School and went on to study engineering at Glasgow University. Like many young men, however, he experienced something of a personal career crisis in his early twenties and, after a year working in a shipyard, enrolled in the Teacher Training course at Jordanhill College in 1925. It was here that his interest

Duncan Macrae as Harry Magog in Bridie's *Gog and Magog*
Courtesy of the Scottish Theatre Archive, University of Glasgow

in acting intensified, when he came in contact with Anne McAllister, who taught Voice Production. Under this influence—which Macrae was always careful to acknowledge in later life—his future became, if not precisely clear, at least determined. Sooner or later, he was going to make his living in the theatre. In the meantime, he became increasingly active in amateur circles and it was in this way that he found his way to Pollock.

It was while acting with the Tron that Macrae received the first important notice of his career. This was for his playing of Soliony in Pollock's 1932 production of Chekhov's *The Three Sisters*. According to James McNair Reid of the *Glasgow Herald* this was 'an immaculate picture of that weird character'. Although the association was not to last long, this would appear to indicate that it was in the crucible of Pollock's rehearsals that Macrae's natural talent was brought to maturity. Technique was never to be Macrae's strong suit—on the contrary, he was often criticised by other actors for his supposed lack of it—but the more adventurous initiatives of his acting were made possible by the safety-net of technique that he had learned from Pollock.

By the following year, however, the Tron Theatre Club was no more, having split into three separate companies. This separation appears to have been brought about over disagreements regarding future policy which were, to the credit of all concerned, concluded without any degree of personal animosity. Although they went their separate ways, all the ex-members of the Tron remained on good terms.

Pollock moved the centre of his operations to Dumbarton, where he eventually established the Scottish People's Theatre, the company which was to become his memorial. After his untimely death in 1938, the SPT survived until the outbreak of war, when it ceased its activities for the duration. After the war, however, interest was revived, the company changed its name to the Dumbarton People's Theatre and, as such, it survives to this day as one of the finest amateur companies in Scotland.

As for Macrae, he took the opportunity to form his own, short-lived company, the Project Theatre. This gave him some valuable directing experience, presenting plays by Paul Vincent Carroll, Cormac Simpson, Hugh MacDiarmid, T M Watson and Emilio Coia. It was his first attempt, albeit on a very small scale, to develop a native Scottish Drama. By October, 1936, however, the Project Theatre had come to an end and Macrae joined forces with the third segment of the disbanded Tron Theatre Club.

Led by Grace Ballantine, Norman Bruce and Molly Urquhart, this group of ex-Tron actors had embarked on an initiative which was to have long-term consequences. In 1933, they established headquarters in the drawing-room of a large house at 15 Woodside Terrace and adopted the name of the Curtain Theatre. Due to the fact that their membership included a wealthy benefactor—John Stewart, their musical director, whose inherited fortune came from a chain of commercial colleges his father had owned in Scotland and the North of England—the Curtain was to initiate a long history. From 1933 until 1935, productions were staged at Woodside Terrace, after which the Curtain moved to the favoured venue of the Scottish National Players and Glasgow Rep: the Lyric in Sauchiehall Street. In 1940, Stewart created a new home for the company at the Park Theatre, hard by the old premises in Woodside Terrace. The Park was a private theatre— the audience restricted to club members—and continued with a fair degree of success until 1949, after which Stewart left Glasgow to concentrate his efforts on a large tent on the banks of the Tummel. The Pitlochry Festival Theatre, the only repertory company in the Highlands, catering mainly for theatre-loving holidaymakers, was the eventual outcome.

All this was very much in the future, of course, and at the beginning the aims of the Curtain were much more idealistic. Like Pollock and Macrae, they were excited by the ideas of the Scottish Renaissance and, in the early years, produced much new Scottish Drama. Among the playwrights they encouraged—which included George Malcolm Thomson, Robins Millar, Donald Mackenzie and Donald McLaren—was the highly individual talent of Robert McLellan.

McLellan was one of a group of young writers who had been directly influenced by Hugh MacDiarmid, particularly with respect to MacDiarmid's efforts to revive the Scots language for serious literary purposes. They believed that Scots possessed latent and under-used qualities which, if released, were capable of obtaining striking new effects. McLellan, whose knowledge and love of Scots was very wide and deep, used the language to paint large-scale, colourful stage pictures which are full of poetry and humour. Most of them draw on elements of Scottish history, but they are not historical plays as such, taking as they do a native contemporary view of episodes in the past.

McLellan's early one-act plays were first performed at Woodside Terrace, but his first full-length drama, *Toom Byres*, was produced at the Lyric in 1936. This was followed, in the 1937 season, by McLellan's finest work for the stage, *Jamie the Saxt*.

Four acts long, with a cast of 20, McLellan's play was the most ambitious work that the Curtain had tackled until then. Grace Ballantine, who was responsible for the first production, immediately realised that the casting of the title rôle would be vital to the play's success. This rôle is the longest and perhaps the most complicated part in the whole corpus of Scottish drama, and there was really only one actor in the company whose talents matched such demands. Despite some opposition from McLellan—who mistakenly believed that a Glasgow upbringing and an Allan Glen's education had deprived him of the ability to speak good Scots—Macrae was cast as the King.

The first production of *Jamie the Saxt*, which took place at the Lyric Theatre in the April of 1937, is now regarded as an important milestone in Scottish dramatic history. It was most certainly a defining moment in Macrae's career. The very length and difficulty of the part—the King is on stage for almost every moment of the entire play—tested his natural resources to the full—and they were not found wanting. Macrae's magnetic stage presence, his detailed sense of gesture, the unique intonation of his voice and his total empathy with McLellan's dramatic vision led to his first really big theatrical success. It was a part he would return to on several occasions throughout his career.

When Macrae first played in *Jamie the Saxt*, however, he was still an amateur, a spare-time actor who worked as a school-teacher during the day. If his success in McLellan's play had convinced him that his future lay in a professional acting career, there remained the severest difficulty in getting started. In those days, it should be remembered, there was simply nowhere in Scotland for a professional actor to work. The reps had not yet been established, while Howard & Wyndham relied almost exclusively on the commercial touring companies. Any aspiring Scottish actor was obliged either to audition in London or to apply for a place in an English rep.

For an actor of Macrae's ambitions, either course would have been pointless and self-defeating. One of his closest associates, Molly Urquhart, an actress whose professional ambitions were equal to his own, had already made such a move. In 1936, after some professional experience with the touring Sheldon Browne rep company at Gourock, she was engaged by the Cambridge Festival Theatre, where she played a number of character rôles in plays by such as Somerset Maugham, Emlyn Williams and Ivor Novello. She had found the experience useful, although somewhat frustrating. As Helen Murdoch has pointed out, in her highly readable account of the Urquhart's life, *Travelling Hopefully* (1981), Scottishness imposed a restriction on her potential range.

> Molly's own voice, though clear and softly modulated, still had Scottish overtones; therefore, she was not considered suitable, in an English company, to play leading rôles either in contemporary dramas, or comedies, or in classic plays.

Macrae would rather have remained an amateur than accept such second-class status. Molly Urquhart, however, was of a much more practical turn of mind. Having polished her acting skills in Cambridge, she returned to Scotland and founded her own company at Rutherglen.

Molly Urquhart's life and career has much in common with that of Duncan Macrae. Approximately the same age—Urquhart was a year younger—they had both been born in Glasgow of Highland parentage, both had begun acting with amateur companies, had studied with Pollock and been influenced by the ideas of the Scottish Renaissance. In the future, both would have successful film careers, which would give them the freedom to make substantial contributions to the new Scottish Theatre.

Although they did not always remain on the best of terms with each other—they had a brother-and-sister kind of relationship and their squabbles became legendary—they both brought much energy and enthusiasm to a common goal.

The Rutherglen company was named after its founder, Mary Sinclair Urquhart, and was known as the MSU. At first, Macrae was sceptical of this venture and refused his support until it had become securely established on a semi-professional basis. In March 1942, he finally laid his reservations aside and gave Urquhart a great deal of valuable support, playing leading rôles in plays by Barrie, St John Ervine, Joe Corrie and, most important of all, James Bridie.

Bridie, of course, is now regarded as the most important single figure in the history of twentieth century Scottish Theatre. There are two reasons for his enduring importance. First, Bridie's great gifts as a dramatist cannot possibly be denied and the best of his plays—*The Anatomist*, *Mr Bolfry* and *The Queen's Comedy*—are among the best that Scottish Drama has to offer. Nor are these plays as dated as is sometimes claimed. As Ivor Brown remarked at the time of Bridie's death in 1951:

> We shall continue to be deliciously plagued with the questions he raised and the an-swers that he did not give. He managed to be an intellectual, and yet to like brave shows, gallantries, ballads, mysteries and nonsense.

That quotation gives a clear indication of the nature of Bridie's importance. Between 1928 and 1951, he wrote 43 stage plays, incorporating 'brave shows, gallantries, ballads, mysteries and nonsense'. In short, at a time when it was desperately needed, James Bridie provided the repertoire of the Scottish Theatre with a degree of *range*—comedies, tragedies, historical drama, biblical plays, fantasies and pantomime are all to be found within the corpus of his output.

Besides being a great dramatist, Bridie was an intensely practical man, a good organiser, a button-holer of the prosperous, a string-puller and a manipulator of committees—and it was in this rôle that he now comes decisively into the story. After resigning in disgust from the board of the Scottish National Players in 1931, Bridie had rather washed his hands of Scotland, concentrating his efforts throughout the '30s on making a place for his drama in the West End. Despite a number of successes there—most notably *The Sleeping Clergyman* (1933) and *Susannah and the Elders* (1937)—he never felt entirely at home in London and, by 1942, his thoughts were turning once more to the idea of creating a Scottish company in Glasgow. Such a theatre would, of course, need the services of Scottish actors, and Bridie, who was well-acquainted with the amateur scene, began to persuade the best of them to 'cut the painter' and turn professional. In July 1943, Bridie's new play, *Mr Bolfry*, was about to go into rehearsal at the Westminster Theatre with Alastair Sim in the leading rôle. Bridie offered Macrae the job of Sim's understudy—for the princely wage of £2:10/- a week—with a promise of a place in the new Glasgow company which was to begin operations in the winter.

Strange to relate, therefore, the professional career of this most Scottish of all modern actors actually began in London—although, as it happened, his presence in Sim's company was short-lived and of a purely token nature. Indeed, only one event of significance took place during the few weeks that Macrae was at the Westminster. At that time, he was accustomed to being billed under his full name, as J D G Macrae. Alastair Sim, a fellow Scot from Edinburgh, thought that this had a most untheatrical ring and suggested that Macrae drop the initials in favour of his second name. It was on his return to Scotland, then, that the name of Duncan Macrae first came before the theatre-going public.

The new company that Macrae joined in the autumn of 1943 was the Glasgow Citizens' Theatre, whose long, distinguished and colourful history continues to this day. It was formed by Bridie, his friend Tom Honeyman (by now the popular Director of Glasgow Art Galleries) and a cinema owner called George Singleton. Although this company was to grow in prominence over the next decade or so, to the point where it came to be regarded as Scotland's unofficial National Theatre, its origins carry a distinct echo of the Glasgow Rep fiasco. Indeed, the very name of the company came from a phrase that Alfred Wareing had used in his first programme note in 1909 (see Chapter 7) and, at least initially, its aims were in no way dissimilar to that of the earlier company. Fortunately for all concerned, James Bridie was no Alfred Wareing.

The Glasgow Citizens' Theatre was more than simply Bridie's creation, it was the fulfillment of a dream he had cherished since the days of the Scottish National Players. Late in 1942, having been appointed to the Scottish committee of CEMA, he set about making this dream a reality with his customary dynamism. He gave a dinner at the Glasgow Arts Club to which he invited everyone he felt could be of use, appointed his directorate, had himself elected Chairman and went round with the hat to collect £1,500 to start the company. From then until his death in 1951, he ran the Glasgow Citizens' like an absolute dictatorship—although he was always diplomatic enough to treat the views of his associates with a measure of respect—and the company, during this time, was very much a reflection of Bridie's preoccupations and prejudices. For instance, determined to avoid amateurism at all costs, he initially ignored the other Scottish companies and went to London for his production staff and most of his cast. Although Macrae's professional career had its true beginning at the Citizens'—first at the Athenaeum and later at the present building in the Gorbals, to which the company moved in 1945—he was one of only three Scots actors who were engaged for the first season—the others being Molly Urquhart and James Gibson—which included only one Scots play, Bridie's *The Holy Isle.*

In time, of course, this was to change and it was during the halcyon days of the Citizens'—from roughly 1945 until the mid-'50s—that the foundations of the new Scottish acting profession were put down most securely. In these years, a whole new generation of Scottish actors cut their teeth at the Citizens': Stanley Baxter, John Cairney and Iain Cuthbertson, among others, made their debuts at this time. Macrae himself played a multitude of contrasting rôles: from a practical Scots Quince in *A Midsummer Night's Dream* to a polished Lord James Stuart in Bridie's *John Knox.* Among them all, however, a number of individual performances stand out as being of particular significance.

The first of these was in in 1944, in Bridie's *The Forrigan Reel*, a pastoral comedy in which Macrae played Donald MacAlpin, the apparently half-witted son of a Highland crofter. This was the part that first revealed Macrae's supreme gift for physical comedy. *The Forrigan Reel* played to capacity audiences in Glasgow for a month, was revived the following summer in Bristol, before going on to Drury Lane and an ENSA tour of France, Belgium, Holland and Germany. There was another revival in 1948, when the Citizens' took the play to Dublin. Gabriel Fallon of the Dublin *Standard* wrote enthusiastically of Macrae's performance.

> The great clowning qualities of Duncan Macrae stand forth as a remarkable feat. His conception of Donald MacAlpin revealed him to be a player of genius. His bodily plastique (to use an American phrase for something rather difficult to define) springing from a personality which rushes to salt his author's sense of humour with his own, marks him out as a master of mime and gesture rarely to be met with in the ranks of a repertory company...

Macrae's performance in *The Forrigan Reel* was a portent of the great comic performances that were to become his stock-in-trade, possibly the most memorable being in Bridie's Christmas Extravaganza *The Tintock Cup*. In time, to the chagrin of a number of his colleagues, he would put these gifts to use more remuneratively in the Variety theatre, starring in some dozen Christmas pantomimes.

Macrae, however, was always much more than simply a gifted clown. He provided clear proof of this in another brilliant performance which took place during the golden era of the Citizens'. This was to involve him in an earth-shaking production in which the modern Scottish Theatre truly came of age: Sir David Lyndsay's *Ane Satyre of the Thrie Estaitis*, presented at the 1948 Edinburgh Festival in an adaptation by Robert Kemp.

Kemp is possibly the most underrated of modern Scottish playwrights. His original plays, although perhaps a little too cosy in their concerns, are models of playwrighting technique. He was always a fine craftsman, and his best work was done in translations and adaptations. Kemp was the first Scottish dramatist to see the possibilities in translating Molière into Scots—which he did to fine effect in his version of *L'École des femmes*, *Let Wives Tak Tent*—creating a tradition which has since been followed by such as Victor Carin, Hector MacMillan and Liz Lochhead. He was also responsible for the brilliant re-working of Isaac Pocock's *Rob Roy* which was a huge hit in the early '60s. Kemp's finest moment, however, came in 1948, with the Lyndsay play, at the second Edinburgh Festival.

In its original form, *Ane Satyre of the Thrie Estaitis*, designed for an all-day performance in the open air, would take something like nine hours to play. Additionally, it is full of obscure topical references which are quite meaningless to modern audiences. Kemp skilfully scaled the play down, modernising the language, yet retaining the original spirit of the piece to such an extent that it is still Kemp's version that is used on the occasions that the play is produced today.

It should be said that the entire conception of the 1948 project—including the use of the Assembly Hall—came from Robert Kemp, although it was Tyrone

Guthrie's superb direction that made the production such a success. Bridie acted as enthusiastic midwife, both in his capacity as Adviser in Drama to the Edinburgh Festival and as Director of the Glasgow Citizens' company, which provided most of the cast. Bryden Murdoch played King Humanitie, Archie Duncan was John the Common Weal, Molly Urquhart was Dame Sensualitie and, snooving and sliding throughout the entire performance, was Duncan Macrae in the double rôle of Flatterie and the Pardoner. At the end of the opening night, as the cast were taking their call, Bridie was heard to mutter 'Now Lord, lettest Thou Thy servant depart in peace'.

His sense of achievement was far from being misplaced. The 1948 production of *The Thrie Estaitis* proved, as never before, that the aspirations of the Scottish Theatre were not, as has often been suggested, simply a question of national vanity, but were motivated by the existence of a distinctive theatrical voice. Further proof of this was provided in the following year, when Macrae gave one of his greatest performances.

Once more, this was in a Bridie play. *Gog and Magog*, based on an actual experience of the Dundee poet William MacGonagall, was originally written on the suggestion of Bridie's secretary, Lindsay Galloway. It was first performed at the Arts Theatre in London in December 1948, with Alec Clunes in the rôle of Harry Magog. In this production, the MacGonagall dimension was ignored and Clunes played the part as a down-at-heel ham actor. The result, while not exactly a failure, made little impact.

When the play was revived at Glasgow Citizens' in 1949, the part of Magog went to Macrae, whose performance transformed the play completely. In the second interval of the opening night, Bridie's biographer Winifred Bannister noticed that the playwright had remained in the foyer when everyone else had taken their seats. Thinking there was something wrong, Bannister approached Bridie and found, sure enough, that there were tears in his eyes. 'I was deeply moved' was all that he said. In her biography, *James Bridie and His Theatre* (Rockcliff, 1955) Bannister recorded this story and made the following comment on the production.

> Duncan Macrae has made the part so superbly his own...he strides unhampered through the melee of the third act, and the curtain seems to come down all too soon on his and Bridie's artistry. To see Duncan Macrae portray this Magog is to experience the genius of Bridie interpreted by genius. Macrae's exquisite balance of comedy and pathos is remarkable. There is no actor living who has a finer sense of timing.

Five years later, Macrae revived the rôle and *Gog and Magog* became the hit of the 1954 Edinburgh Festival, playing to full houses of 2,000 people every night for three weeks.

This, however, was not a Glasgow Citizens' production. In 1952, Macrae had formed his own company, Scottishows, in partnership with the populist Scots playwright, T M Watson. Accounts of the first tours of Scottishows call to mind the golden era of the Victorian actor-manager. Macrae toured the country from Inverness to Hawick—and across the border to Carlisle—playing to huge audiences everywhere.

T M Watson, like Joe Corrie, had long been established as a professional playwright who made his living from writing for the amateur stage, and the first two plays were from his pen: *Bachelors are Bold* and *Johnny Jouk the Gibbet*, honest Scots comedies with a mass popular appeal, in which Macrae could exploit his comic talents. It was only after a secure base had been established that Macrae took the calculated risk of *Gog and Magog*. The following year, a new Scots play was produced: Alexander Reid's *The World's Wonder*, in which Macrae played the part of the wizard, Michael Scott. At Edinburgh's leading Variety house, the Palladium, this play broke all records, drawing no fewer than 31,154 people in the course of its run, 6,000 more than any other play in that year's Festival. One cannot fail to notice the sense of satisfaction in a remark that Macrae made in a press interview at the time: 'One of the main criticisms levelled against Scots plays is that no one goes to see them anyway. I have tried to make that particular criticism invalid.'

Although this was certainly no idle boast, there is a sense in which Macrae was over-simplifying the situation. The fact is that the drive towards a Scottish Theatre was now so logical that it had become irresistible, even to those who had initially been indifferent to the concept. For instance, Glasgow Unity Theatre, which Macrae had been tempted to join in 1940, had a commitment to World Theatre and, despite the presence of its resident playwright, James Barke, tended to avoid native drama—the sole reason why Macrae, who otherwise shared Unity's politics, had refused to join—yet its most famous production, an enormous hit in 1948, was a play set in contemporary Glasgow by a Scottish author: *The Gorbals Story* by Robert McLeish.

By this time, then, it had become clear that the Scottish Theatre was in the midst of a great revival. Apart from his work at Glasgow Citizens', Bridie had been instrumental in founding a new drama college for Scottish actors, at the Royal Scottish Academy of Music. The first students enrolled in 1950 and, within a few years, would be applying for work at the Citizens' and the other Scottish reps which, as we have seen, were increasingly developing a more indigenous profile. As if this were not enough, the community of Scottish theatres was joined in 1953 by a new company which had been formed in Edinburgh with a specific commitment to Scottish drama.

The Gateway Theatre was born in the most unusual circumstances. In 1946, the Church of Scotland inherited an empty building, a former cinema, at the top of Leith Walk. This was a most unexpected acquisition and at first the Church was at a complete loss as to what to do with it. Quite remarkably, the decision was taken to establish a repertory company in the building, which the Church had renamed the Gateway. A young minister, the Rev. George Candlish, was put in charge of the operation and, with the help of Robert Kemp and others, Candlish managed the theatre for the next few years as a purely business enterprise, providing a venue for a number of ad hoc companies, sometimes professional but usually amateur. Then, in 1948, the Glasgow Citizens' paid a short visit to Edinburgh to give a performance of Kemp's *Let Wives Tak Tent*, with Duncan Macrae in the rôle of Oliphant. This was so successful that Candlish became convinced that a regular professional company could be established at the Gateway and approached Kemp with an invitation to form such a company.

Between 1953 and 1965, the Gateway presented 158 individual productions, 94 of them by Scottish authors, plus a number of others—Bjornson's *Mary Stuart in Scotland*, for instance—which had strong Scottish associations. It represented every aspect of Scottish drama, not only giving opportunities to new Scottish playwrights such as A D Mackie, Maurice Fleming and R J B Sellar, but reaching back into the past to present plays by Aimee Stuart, J M Barrie, Graham Moffat and even managing to revive—through the good offices of Robert Kemp—the old warhorse, *Rob Roy*. With a company that included such names as Tom Fleming, Lennox Milne, Nell Ballantyne, Victor Carin, Sheila Donald, Michael Elder, Marillyn Gray, Edith MacArthur, Michael O'Halloran, Marjorie Thomson and John Young, it was a vibrant addition to the Scottish theatrical community and a popular feature of Edinburgh life. It was a company which came to an end, moreover, not through any loss of energy or absence of popularity, but simply because the subsidies it received from Edinburgh Corporation and the Scottish Arts Council were required elsewhere.

The experience of the Gateway is emblematic of its period, for it was in the mid-'50s that the Scottish Theatre was cut down at the very height of its triumph. Television, of course, was the culprit, particularly after the granting of the ITV franchises in 1956. This not only had a disastrous effect on audience levels, but actually changed the whole nature of theatre-going. Before television, the theatre was regarded as a public facility, supported by regular playgoers certainly, but essentially an integral part of the general life of the community. After the arrival of television, theatre quickly assumed the rôle of a minority interest. This notion was reinforced by the increasing part played by the funding bodies in theatrical activity.

For those professionally involved, it had become obvious that the theatre would never be the same again. Wilson Barrett, who had seen the writing on the wall as early as 1955, closed down his company and retired from management. (Significantly enough, his last appearance in Edinburgh was at the Gateway in a Scottish play, *Heather on Fire* by Moray McLaren.) Duncan Macrae, too, could see what was coming and wound up Scottishows at the same time. Like Barrett, Macrae's company had been completely self-financing and received no public subsidy of any kind, although a measure of subsidy was enjoyed in the form of Macrae's lucrative film career. In all, he made some 18 films and the best of these—notably *The Brothers* (1947) and *The Kidnappers* (1953)—reveal a natural aptitude for the medium. There is little doubt that, had he chosen, he could have deserted the theatre for a career in films.

But Duncan Macrae could not desert either the theatre or Scotland. In the years ahead, he would make several journeys south of the border to play interesting rôles. He appeared with Laurence Olivier in Ionesco's *Rhinoceros* at the Royal Court Theatre in 1960, was one of the original cast of Joe Orton's *Loot* in 1965, and played Molière's Harpagon in *L'Avare* at the Mermaid Theatre in 1966. These performances aside, however, his loyalties always remained in Scotland and at the time of his death in 1967—at the comparatively early age of 61—he was rehearsing the part of Long John Silver in Stevenson's *Treasure Island* at the Royal Lyceum Theatre in Edinburgh, which had become a fully-subsidised theatre two years earlier, in 1965.

Macrae's life ended with a suddenness that shocked and stunned the entire Scottish community. It transpired that this most vital of actors had been unknowingly harbouring a cancerous brain tumour which entered its terminal stage with devastating speed. He collapsed at his Glasgow home on 1 December, 1966 and, after just three months of hospital confinement, he passed away on the 23 March, 1967. Tributes poured in from all over the country and the streets were lined for his funeral at Linn Crematorium. As far as the theatrical community, in particular, was concerned, the profound sadness was deepened by the thought that, much as he had achieved, he might have achieved so much more. The best that could be said was that he had died when he was still at the height of his powers.

The death of Macrae, untimely as it was, seems an appropriate place to bring this history to an end. Apart from any other consideration, the history of the subsidised theatre in Scotland is part of a different history—involving film, radio and television—and must be viewed in a quite different context. All that needs to be said at this point is that the injection of public funds, which were granted with the intention of creating a degree of artistic liberation, has only succeeded in leading the Scottish Theatre into a dead end.

The last 30 years have not, of course, been without noteworthy incident. In this connection, one immediately thinks of Bill Bryden's work at the Lyceum in the early '70s, Chris Parr's inspired management of the Traverse a few years later, the heroic efforts of Ewan Hooper and Tom Fleming to establish the Scottish Theatre Company, Giles Havergal's masterly direction of Glasgow Citizens' and the great proliferation of theatre at two important festivals: Glasgow's Mayfest and the Edinburgh Festival Fringe. The theatre in Scotland today is, in many ways, more versatile, more outward-looking and, in some respects at least, more artistically adventurous than it used to be.

The fact remains, however, that the *rôle* of theatre within our society has become gradually diminished, in terms of both influence and scope. Audiences are not only smaller, they are less representative; production values may be higher but the productions themselves are less ambitious; managements may be in possession of more resources—both financial and artistic—but they are much more reticent in making use of them. All things considered, it would be reasonable to assume that the art of theatre in Scotland is currently in a state of terminal decline.

Yet, if the experience of the last 250 years has taught us anything, it is that the theatre re-invents itself every generation or so. Drama fulfils a number of basic human needs, the most important of which is the need to gain a perspective on existence. Shakespeare's 'mirror up to nature' allows us to come to terms with the most pressing issues of daily life, the follies of our remembered past and the hopes of our imagined future. This need, of course, can be served just as appropriately—some would argue more appropriately—by the electronic media. There is another human need, however, which is likely to grow more urgent in the future: the need to congregate, to identify, to form a community. So many manifestations of modern life—the television, the motor car, the personal computer—conspire to deprive us of the means to satisfy this need that, sooner or later, some kind of mass reaction in the opposite direction is bound to take place. For this reason alone, some kind of theatrical renewal is inevitable.

Just as the old Scottish stage had to give way to the English actor-managers, as the actor-managers had to give way to repertory, repertory to subsidy, so will subsidy in its turn be obliged to give way to some unknown theatrical form of the future. Whatever form that takes will be decided, not by the funding bodies, not by the worthy and well-meaning ladies and gentlemen who serve on theatre boards, not even by leading actors like Macrae—whose talents will always find a stage somewhere or other—but by a group of men and women on whom the theatre has always had to depend for its very existence. The future of the Scottish Theatre will be shaped, as the past has been shaped, by the Scottish acting community.

Epilogue

THE COMMON PLAYER

In the late '70s, a casual visitor to Edinburgh's Traverse Theatre—then situated in the Grassmarket—might have been surprised by the sight of an elderly lady playing the fruit-machine in the bar. In age and appearance, she looked distinctly out of place, her cloth coat and Sunday bonnet, hand-bag, worsted stockings and sensible shoes clashing with the casual colour of that youthful milieu. One might easily be forgiven for thinking that an errant member of the local Woman's Guild had strayed into the Traverse by accident. It would be something of a surprise to be told that this was one of the most popular and well-respected figures in the Scottish Theatre, the former manager of the Gateway—Miss Sadie Aitken MBE.

On the face of it, Sadie Aitken's contribution to the Scottish Theatre was as an organiser and administrator. She was involved with the Scottish Community Drama Association from the very start, gaining election to its General Council and serving on numerous committees. She was manager of the Gateway for the entirety of its existence and, when the Church sold the building to Scottish Television, she became Festival Manager at St Cecilia's Hall and, for a short time, was in charge of the Church's new theatrical acquisition, the Netherbow in the High Street. She was an astute and able manager, with a deep understanding of her potential audience and a sure touch in predicting success or failure at the box-office. For instance, she once predicted that Ada F Kay's fine play *The Man from Thermopylae*, would not get the audience it deserved because Edinburgh people, unsure of how to pronounce the title, would be embarrassed about booking. Unfortunately, this prediction proved all too accurate.

For all her administrative abilities, however, Sadie Aitken was always, at heart, an actor. A born raconteur, with immaculate timing and a droll, ready wit, she was capable of holding any company in thrall with her fund of theatrical stories. Performance always delighted her and she relished even the smallest rôles. In 1928, as an aspiring young amateur, she was briefly hired by Robert

Fenemore's Masque Theatre to play a tiny part in some long-forgotten play. There was only one line—'I feel sick'—but Sadie managed to wring every last nuance out of it. 'It was wonderful' she told the present author 50 years later, 'I said it differently every single night!' Her Equity card was one of her proudest possessions and, in her declining years, she satisfied her passion for acting by working as a TV extra. For all who loved her, the sight of Sadie entering Isobel Blair's shop in an episode of STV's *Take the High Road*, screened some weeks after her death in 1985, was a very moving experience indeed.

Sadie Aitken may not have been a great actor, but she was a *real* actor. This is a term for which Wilson Barrett, in *On Stage for Notes*, gave the following definition.

> When I say 'real actor', I don't mean good actor or bad actor, success or failure, but simply the men and women who love the theatre so much that they will suffer any hardship so long as they can be part of it. This driving power gives them the strength to cope with hardship and poverty...they devote their whole lives to the theatre.

There have been many such actors in the Scottish Theatre over the years. One of them was Kitty de Legh, a Wilson Barrett regular, who went straight to rehearsal from the funeral of her husband, Caleb Porter, in 1940. Kitty left the Barrett company in 1941 to work for the BBC, but two years later, when Barrett, desperately short of cast, tentatively asked her to return, she replied with a telegram that is worth quoting:

YES DARLING ANY TIME YOU LIKE HURRAH HURRAH HURRAH

Such actors have also been found in the Amateur Theatre. One such is Elspet Cameron who, though she has often worked professionally, is an amateur in the best sense of the word—there is no more devoted or dedicated lover of the art of theatre in Scotland. A member of Glasgow Unity, Elspet played the part of Nurse White in Unity's 1946 production of Ena Lamont Stewart's *Starched Aprons* and later carried a broom in Tyrone Guthrie's original production of *Ane Satyre of the Thrie Estaitis*. At the time of writing, she is still active, appearing in television dramas and commercials, besides buzzing all over Scotland, giving her support to as many theatres as possible. (In 1995, Elspet found herself in hospital at a time when the students at the RSAMD were reviving *Starched Aprons*. Nothing daunted, she persuaded the hospital authorities to part with an ambulance and a wheelchair in order that she could be at the opening!) A fine reader of verse, she has long been associated with the Scottish Poetry Society, for which she has given many readings.

In the days before repertory became established, there was an actor in Edinburgh called John Perry, who kept the stage-door at the Lyceum for 40 years, until his retiral in 1920. He had been given this job by J B Howard who, knowing Perry's dislike of touring, had taken the opportunity of keeping a first-class actor in the theatre. Perry appeared frequently with the Howard & Wyndham Players and was a great favourite, not only of the 'stage-door johnnies', but of the many celebrities that visited Edinburgh. When Ellen Terry paid her last visit to Edinburgh in 1906, she greeted her old friend with a quotation from *Much Ado About Nothing*, the first play to be performed on the Lyceum stage. 'Dear John Perry!' cried the great actress, paraphrasing Benedick's first line to Beatrice, 'Are you yet living?'

In the 1870s, when John Perry was just beginning his stage career, an old actor called George Fisher was still playing in Edinburgh. A comedian in the Mackay tradition, Fisher had, in his youth, acted with the great Henry Erskine Johnston. At the high point of his career, he had played Bailie Nicol Jarvie in a production of *Rob Roy* in which the part of Rashleigh Osbaldistone had been played by the promising young Henry Irving. In his time, George Fisher had played the Waverley Dramas all over the world. Now in very much reduced circumstances, he was giving the final performances of his life on the stage of a penny gaff in the Cowgate. He would continue acting until the day he died.

In days of the old Theatre Royal, of course, there were many such actors, none more so than a rather interesting, if slightly mysterious, character named Power, who played under Murray's management for over 20 years. Although his first name is unknown, this actor is not to be confused with his more famous contemporary, the great-grandfather of Tyrone Guthrie and the film-star: it is no more than a coincidence that Tyrone Power was appearing on the Scottish stage at approximately the same time. Murray's Power was something of a ruffian, who was frequently in trouble with the police, and who died in the Royal Infirmary in 1843, from wounds sustained in a drunken brawl. He was very popular, however, particularly in Scottish rôles and, although Murray no doubt disapproved of Power's extramural activities, he considered him invaluable.

The kind of popularity that Power enjoyed was not, however, the variety of which stars are made. He was what was then known as a 'gallery' actor, his following being largely confined to the cheap seats. Another gallery favourite was Paddy Weekes of the Ryder company, an Irish actor and singer who had a particular following in Perth. In October, 1838, Weekes was travelling from Glasgow to Perth when he was involved in a terrible accident. In thick fog, the coach left the road and overturned, much of its weight descending on Weekes. Although no bones were broken, the bruising was so serious that he did not survive for more than a few weeks. Ryder immediately arranged a benefit for his wife and children, which raised the sum of £60—a remarkable sum, when one considers that a full house at Perth Theatre Royal would, in those days, usually draw no more that £32. This is a measure of his popularity, as is the stone which was placed over his grave in Greyfriars Burying Ground, Perth—bearing the date and one single word, WEEKES.

Most actors, of course, can expect little more in the way of a memorial—but there have been exceptions. The oldest and possibly most attractive playhouse in Scotland is the Theatre Royal, Dumfries, founded in 1792, largely through the efforts of George Stephens Sutherland, a former member of John Jackson's company who had settled in the town. Associated with Sutherland in this enterprise was the poet Robert Burns, who wrote a number of prologues and helped engage Alexander Nasmyth to paint the first stage sets. 'A worthier or cleverer fellow I have rarely met with', Burns wrote of the actor and, apart from the fact that his was a popular and successful management, this is almost all that is known of Sutherland's character. The Theatre Royal, however, survives to this day as an enduring memorial to his popularity.

In the earliest days of the Scottish Theatre, when actors had to deal with indifference and hostility, such popularity was rarely available, but even then it was not completely unknown. In 1752, a small wooden booth was set up near Glasgow Cathedral for the use of a visiting company from Edinburgh, and met with so much hostility that the actors had to be physically protected. One of these actors was Francis Stamper, a comedian and satirist of such skill that he eventually won the audience over. For the next ten years, Stamper maintained a large following in Edinburgh and Glasgow and, when he died in 1766, George Stayley (of the Stayley Riot fame) penned the following epitaph.

> Is Stamper dead? He is—to all below.
> Look in each face—you'll read it in their woe!
> He who was wont to raise the general smile,
> And for whole nights a world of care beguile:
> (Oh sudden change!)—whence comes it, Stamper, now,
> You fix such gloomy sorrow on the brow?
> 'Forgive my son'—the comic genius cry'd:
> He never grieved a soul; but when he died.

Frank Stamper, George Stephens Sutherland, Paddy Weekes, Power, George Fisher, John Perry, Elspet Cameron, Kitty de Legh and Sadie Aitken, names that have been chosen more or less at random—to which dozens more could have been added—have played as full a part in the making of the Scottish Theatre as any of their more distinguished colleagues. As Hugh MacDiarmid once wrote, 'to raise a wave to a maximum crest requires all the weight of the ocean's waters'. In the theatre, it is the common player who supplies the weight; they have created the past, and their counterparts, today, tomorrow and the day after that, will fashion the future. If there is no audience, they will create one; if money is short, they will make do with what there is; every difficulty, no matter how forbidding, will be overcome by their obsessive compulsion to perform, a compulsion they will serve whatever the cost.

For most actors, this can only be done with any degree of satisfaction on the stage of a theatre. The great drawback of radio, television and film, as far as acting is concerned, is that every performance in these media is, as the Americans say, a one-shot deal. Only in the theatre is the actor free to explore and develop a character over a succession of performances, to return to the same character, perhaps after several years, to play it again, from a completely new angle. It is for this reason that most actors like to say that they belong to the theatre.

This notion is totally false, of course. Actors do not belong to the theatre; in fact, it is the opposite that is true—it is the theatre that belongs to them.

BIBLIOGRAPHY

Library Sources
National Library of Scotland
Edinburgh Room, Edinburgh Central Library
Scottish Theatre Archive, Glasgow
People's Palace, Glasgow
Scottish Record Office

Manuscript
Armstrong, Norma, *The Edinburgh Stage, 1715-1820* (A Fellowship Thesis for the Library Association 1968, on deposit in Edinburgh Room)

Books and Articles
Angus, J Keith, *A Scotch Playhouse* (Aberdeen, 1878)
Bannister, Winifred, *James Bridie and his Theatre* (London, 1955)
Barlow, Priscilla, *Wise Enough to Play the Fool* (Edinburgh, 1995)
Barrett, Wilson, *On Stage for Notes* (Edinburgh, 1954)
Baynham, G W, *History of the Glasgow Stage* (Glasgow, 1892)
Bolton, H Philip, *Scott Dramatized* (London, 1992)
Boyd, Frank, *Records of the Dundee Stage* (Dundee, 1886)
Campbell, Donald, *A Brighter Sunshine* (Edinburgh, 1983)
Corrie, Joe, *Poems, Plays and Theatre Writings* (ed. Linda Mackenney, Glasgow, 1983)
Dibdin, J C, *Annals of the Edinburgh Stage* (Edinburgh, 1888)
Donaldson, Walter, *Recollections of an Actor* (London, 1865)
Downs, Harold (ed.), *Theatre and Stage* (London, 1932)
Ffrench, Yvonne, *Mrs Siddons* (London, 1936)
Genest, John, *Some Account of the English Stage* (London, 1832)
Guthrie, Tyrone, *A Life in the Theatre* (London, 1960)
Hardwicke, Cedric, *Let's Pretend* (London, 1932)
Highfill, Philip H A et al., *A Biographical Dictionary of Actors, Actresses, Musicians, Dancers, Managers and Other Stage Personnel in London, 1660-1800* (Carbondale, Ill., USA, 1973)

Hutchison, Alison, *Corrie in Cardenden* (Edinburgh, 1986)

Hutchison, David, *The Modern Scottish Theatre* (Glasgow, 1977)

Irving, Laurence, *Henry Irving: The Actor and his World* (London, 1951)

Jackson, John, *A History of the Scottish Stage* (Edinburgh, 1793)

Kemp, Robert, et al, *The Twelve Seasons of the Edinburgh Gateway Company 1953-1965* (Edinburgh, 1965)

Lawson, Robb, *The Story of the Scottish Stage* (Paisley, 1917)

Littlejohn, J H, *The Scottish Music Hall 1880-1990* (Wigtown, 1990)

Mackenzie, Donald, *Scotland's First National Theatre* (Edinburgh, 1963)

Macleod, Joseph, 'Allan Ramsay: The Fight for his Theatre', *Scotsman*, 22-24 April, 1954

Mavor, Ronald, *Dr. Mavor and Mr. Bridie* (Edinburgh, 1988)

Mellor, G J, *The Northern Music Hall* (Newcastle, 1970)

Moffat, Graham, *Join Me in Remembering* (London, 1955)

Murdoch, Helen, *Travelling Hopefully; The Story of Molly Urquhart* (Edinburgh, 1981)

Murray, W H, *Addresses to the Theatre Royal* (Edinburgh, 1851)

Nicol, Allardyce, *History of the English Drama 1660-1900* (Cambridge, 1955)

Pope, W Macqueen, *Haymarket: Theatre of Perfection* (London, 1948)

Stanislavsky, K, *Building a Character* (London, 1949)

INDEX

Buchanan, Nell 102
Buckram in Armour 11, 16
Bulloch, J M 69
Bunty Pulls the Strings 97, 98
Burke and Hare 90
Burns, Robert 32, 100, 142
Byre Theatre Company, St Andrews 121, 122

Cairney, John 133
Calcraft, J W 47, 48, 74
Caledonia 37
Caledonian Theatre, Edinburgh 26, 28, 36, 53, 54, 55, 64, 65, 66, 67
Caledonian Theatre, Glasgow 73, 74, 76, 77
Cameron, Elspet 141, 143
Campbell, Mrs Patrick 115
Campbell, Willie 84, 87
Candlish, Rev George 136, 137
Canongate Theatre, Edinburgh 8, 18, 29, 31, 59, 72, 73
Careless Husband, The 11
Carin, Victor 134, 137
Carlyle, Alexander, of Inveresk 2, 18
Caroline of Brunswick 22
Carr, Walter 117
Carroll, Paul Vincent 127
Carrubber's Close 2, 9, 10, 11, 13, 14, 16, 17
Cathleen ni Houlihan 92
Causey Saints 95, 96, 97, 98
Cazabon, Albert 95
Chapin, Harold 95
Charles XII 39
Cheats of Scapin, The 2
Cibber, Theophilus 9
Citizens' Theatre, Glasgow 107, 109, 110, 133, 134-138
City Theatre, Glasgow 79, 86
Clark, Jamieson 117
Clewlow, Frank 101
Clunes, Alec 135
Clyde, Andy 89
Clyde, David 89
Clyde, Jean 89
Clyde, John 89
Colin in Fairyland 95
Colman the Younger, George 59
Compton, Edward 88, 112
Concealed Bed, The 92, 96
Conscious Lovers, The 31
Cooke's Circus 79
Coriolanus 52, 61
Corri, Natali 25, 26, 36, 64

Corrie, Joe vii, 90, 99, 103, 104-111
Cowell, Joe 35
Cowell, Sam 35,87
Coy Shepherdess, The 4
Cramond Brig 56
Crawford, Andrew 127
Crawford, Neil 117
Cruikshank, A Stewart 115
Curtain Theatre, Glasgow 129, 130
Cuthbertson, Iain 133

de Legh, Kitty 141, 143
Defoe, Daniel 72
Dence, Marjorie 119, 120, 122, 123
Denham, Edward 48
Derby, Brown 117
Despard, Charlotte 92
Dibdin, J C 4, 6, 11, 18, 59, 66, 77
Die Frieschutz 76
Digges, West 18, 30, 31, 32, 41
Dillon, Charles 70
Dobson, Helen 91
Dolmetsch Orchestra 115
Dominion of Fancy 76, 77
Donald, Sheila 137
Douglas 17, 18, 20, 49, 74
Dragon 62
Drummond, George 4-5, 6, 7, 8
Ducrow, Andrew 77
Duff, Albert 48
Dumfries Guild of Players 100
Duncan, Archie 117, 135
Dundas, Robert 23, 33
Dundee Dramatic Society 120
Dundee Repertory Theatre 120, 121, 122
Dunfermline Opera House 105
Dunlop Street Fire Panic 79-80
Dunlop, James, of Garnkirk 72
Dyall, Franklin 95
Dyke, Ann 42

Earl of Essex, The 31
Earl of Lauderdale 6
Edinburgh Company of Players 8, 9, 10, 13, 29
Edinburgh Equestrian Circus 21, 25
Elder, Michael 137
Election, The 24
Elibank, Lord Patrick et al 29, 30, 38, 72
Empire Theatre, Edinburgh 116
Empress Music Hall, Glasgow 96
Erskine of Tinwald 13